*Gardening with Stone and Sand*

# Gardening with Stone and Sand

by JACK KRAMER

Botanical Plates by

MICHAEL VALDEZ and CHARLES HOEPPNER

Garden Plans by FRANK A. CHIN LOY

CHARLES SCRIBNER'S SONS
New York

Copyright © 1972 Jack Kramer

This book published simultaneously in the United States of America and in Canada — Copyright under the Berne Convention

All rights reserved. No part of this book may be reproduced in any form without the permission of Charles Scribner's Sons.

Printed in the United States of America

# Contents

Introduction: THE QUIET GARDEN     viii

1. THE BEAUTY OF STONE     1
   The "Dry Garden"
   Gardens of Stones and Plants
   Selecting Stones
   Designing with Stones
   Arranging Stones
   How to Handle Stones

2. THE BEAUTY OF SAND, GRAVEL, AND OTHER MATERIALS     10
   Sand
   Gravel
   Grades of Gravel
   Cobble
   Crushed Stone
   Other Materials

3. PLANNING THE STONE AND SAND GARDEN     17
   Planning on Paper
   The Garden Design
   Making It Work

4. PLANTS FOR STONE AND SAND GARDENING    26
   Plant Material
   Care of Plants
   How to Use Plants
   List of Shrubs
   List of Trees
   Flowering Fruit Trees: Cherry, Plum
   Flowering Plants
   The Rockery or Mound Garden

5. DWARF PLANTS AND GROUND COVERS    49
   Dwarf Conifer Trees
   List of Dwarf Conifer Trees
   List of Dwarf Evergreen Shrubs
   Ground Covers
   List of Ground Covers

6. POPULAR STONE AND SAND GARDEN PLANTS    58
   Bamboo
   List of Bamboos
   Azaleas
   Care of Azaleas
   List of Azaleas
   Pines
   List of Pines
   Chamaecyparis
   List of Chamaecyparis

7. PATHS AND STEPPING-STONES    70
   Simple Paths
   Stepping-Stones
   Installing Stepping-Stones

8. WATER IN THE GARDEN            76
   Pools and Ponds
   Plants for Water Gardens
   Plants Around the Pool
   Floating Plants for the Pool
   Water Lilies
   Ways to Suggest Water in the Garden

9. MAINTENANCE AND PEST CONTROL       83
   Plant Protection
   Protection against Insects

# Introduction: The Quiet Garden

Although we all want beautiful gardens, often we don't have the time to care for them. A garden of trees and shrubs requires work; so does a flower garden. There are weeding, pruning, mowing, planting, and transplanting. For people with time this is a fine kind of garden, but for those who do not have time, nature is still available at your doorstep—and no less diminished in beauty—in gardens of stone and sand. Here, there are only a few plants (if any), and, once materials are in place, the stone and sand garden takes care of itself.

American gardeners have always had a keen eye on Japanese landscapes, and this is especially true at the present time. We all yearn for closeness with nature and need a place of quiet and repose. We need a setting for our home that is simple and restrained, yet beautiful. The Japanese have ably captured these moods in their gardens of stone and sand. And we can simulate and adapt these ideas to our mode of life. American suppliers now offer an incredible array of stones, pebbles, and sand for the quiet garden.

A Japanese garden depends on space and mass; space is used as a design element. Consider a pruned tree; it is the spaces between the branches that make it a sculptural gem. In the stone and sand garden, trees and shrubs are used sparingly, flowers only occasionally. Air, water, stone, and space are the garden's main components. This is a good premise and especially useful today, for many trees and shrubs are dying because of polluted air.

In this book we do not want, nor should we try, to copy Japanese gardens. We do, however, want to use the concept of stone, rock, gravel, and sand in planning our own landscapes. We want to use these materials on our own terms, for our mode of living is quite different from that of the Japanese.

In stone, sand, and gravel, nature waits to be molded into an attractive natural garden. You have at your fingertips textures of infinite values, colors of incredible beauty, and forms without equal. Combined with a few choice plants, the stone and sand garden can be a satisfying, attractive setting. It may not be blatantly showy, but its quiet beauty speaks loudly to all who see it.

*Jack Kramer*

# 1. The Beauty of Stone

In nature many of the most beautiful landscapes have stones or pebbles thrusting from the earth; stone and plants and earth have been thrown together in a marvelous way to create an appealing picture. A stone may be a large rock or a boulder, a pebble, a cobble, or gravel. (The word *stone* encompasses all these forms.) In natural landscapes, stone groupings are always attractive, as though meticulously arranged by an unseen hand. Nature is a master designer, and from her we can learn much that we can apply to our own personal garden.

Stones are strong visual design elements in any garden; they give weight and dimension and blend plants and earth together. They also give scale to a setting, and once in place they require little maintenance. Indeed, they become more beautiful as they weather through the years.

Stones arranged in the garden should appear as if they have been there for years; they must seem natural in their placement. Rocks and boulders are the dominant framework of the garden and gravel and sand complement the setting.

A stone garden depends on a gentle kind of beauty, although the beauty is partially hidden. This garden works on the imagination and so requires something of the viewer. It presents just enough interest to command attention, but never so much that it is overpowering. In some ways this garden has an aura of mystery; as with all good mysteries, we study it to solve it. This is the garden of repose, and it

*A trio of stones at the corner of this entrance is the balance for the solitary rock in the center of the gravel area. Plantings are carefully chosen—low, hardly ostentatious, yet perfectly in mood with the character of the house. One large tree in the distance serves as a focal point.* Photo by Hedrich Blessing.

may be called somber, subtle, or elegant, depending on composition. It not only delights the eye; it feeds the soul solace and calm.

The "Dry Garden"

The "dry garden"—stone and sand—is austere and simple. Its beauty depends on the arrangement of the materials, and its execution is never easy. For many homes this scene is too stark and too austere, and its character may not be in keeping with the style of the home. Yet I have seen it used effectively with contemporary architecture in courtyards and entries.

The garden without plants relies on muted colors and restraint. In its Japanese context it is a garden of symbolism: a body of water, a canyon, or other natural scene. This is a garden for shady places where grass and plants will not, or are not able to, grow. It is suitable for side yards, northern locations, and other problem areas.

A "dry garden" can be installed practically fully developed. However, it does need routine care: weeds must be kept out of the garden, and blowing leaves and other debris must always be removed quickly.

*A few rocks create a dry garden at the entrance to this house. Note imbedded cobbles in the pavement to complete the scene. Photo by author.*

## Gardens of Stones and Plants

The plant and stone garden, like the "dry garden," approaches beauty through symmetry and understatement. It can blend with almost any type of architecture without hindering the total scene. Of course, like all good landscapes, it must be in proportion to the overall picture; it can be neither too large nor too small, for it must fit.

This garden, with its stones and selected plants, combines an informal look with a formal undercurrent. It is never brash or overpowering, but always in good taste. Although it can be created with existing plants, it is better to start from scratch, so that you have absolute control of what goes into the garden. Every plant and stone must be selected carefully to create the beauty that is inherent in such a landscape.

With gardens of stone and plants, maintenance is minimal; once the picture is set, it needs only routine care; this includes pruning and training of trees and shrubs, and clearing away leaves from gravel and stone areas.

## Selecting Stones

Very few properties will have enough natural stones to work with, and there are very few places where you can randomly collect stones. In fact, many areas have laws prohibiting removal of any natural material, so you may have to order stones from suppliers.

Stone, sand, gravel, and cobble can be purchased at building supply houses or garden material centers. (Check the classified section of your local phone book.) There are innumerable kinds, sizes, shapes, and colors of stone, and in most cases the supplier will let you choose your individual stones. Take your time to find the right ones.

Generally, stone comes in shades of gray or earthy brown, and these are superlative colors for garden work. Avoid brightly colored stones, unless they are native to your area. With gravel there are several different sizes; color varies from a milky-gray to a dark gray. (See next chapter.) Cobble is usually gray or black, often rounded, but recently I have seen flat cobble-typed stones as well. Sand, too, comes in many colors and sizes. Beware of fine sand (it will blow away in the garden) and of white sand (it causes glare in sun). Inspect materials before you buy, so that you get the right kind for the project you have in mind.

Don't select a hodgepodge of different kinds of stone, but rather stick to one kind so there is unity in the garden. Stone shapes vary considerably, and it is quite all right to use smooth-edged stones and sharp-edged ones in the same landscape. But restrict one kind of stone to each individual grouping; do not mix them.

Study the rocks from different angles to be sure that they are interesting and have some character. Seek the unusual—the ones with interesting crevices or textures and, if you can find them, the ones that have moss or lichen on them.

At most supply yards you will also find Featherock and Lavarock—lightweight stones about one-fifth the weight of natural stone. Featherock comes in shades of gray and is not an artificial stone; it is quarried in northern California. Lavarock comes in earthy reds and black. Both materials are satisfactory and can be used effectively in the stone and sand garden.

### Designing with Stones

Sometimes a single large boulder can be the center of attention, as in the garden with stones that complement each other placed around the boulder. Always select stones for their individual character and for their ability to work with plants.

Too many stones give too much weight and bulk to the design; but stones are dominant and should not be lost among the plants. A variance of size is necessary to give the composition rhythm and vitality. Remember to balance greenery with stone, so that harmony exists between both elements.

Avoid perfectly round stones or boulders; seek irregular shapes and a variety of surfaces. You are working with mass and form, so avoid using groupings that are the same general shape and size. Train your eye to seek the unusual stone or boulder that is interesting to view and that will blend well with other elements.

There are five basic stone shapes. The low, rounded form is almost like a mound, with sides that angle out broadly at the base. This shape gives mass and horizontal accent. The reclining form is two to three times as broad as its height and has peaks and valleys. How-

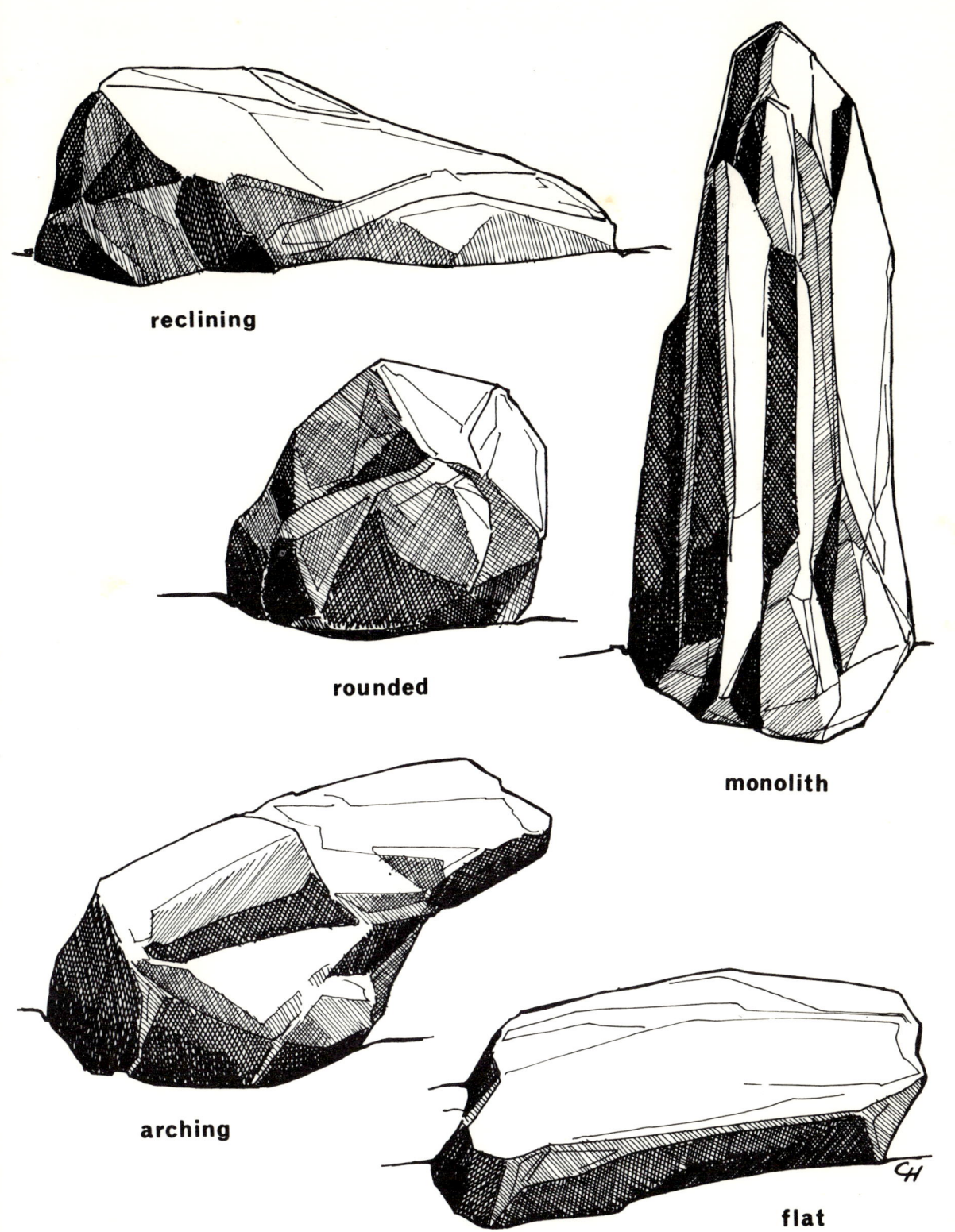

**ROCK SHAPES**

ever, it is basically still a low mass and thus blends well with gravel islands or water areas.

The irregular or arching form is much less symmetrical than either the tall or low form. Its base is generally broader than its top, but slight overhangs and deep ravines are attractive. It can stand alone as a feature or can be used with flat-form stepping-stones.

The flat form stone is broad and flat-topped; it is neither massive nor does it make a statement. It is ground-hugging and stable in feeling. It can be used for paths or to accompany reclining stones.

The tall, standing form (monolith) is two or three times taller than its width. It thrusts itself from the earth and is a dramatic, exciting force, but it must be securely anchored so that it will not topple. It can be used alone, but looks better with low, rounded stones near it.

The force of a stone depends on its shape and how the eye travels when it views it. Some stones, by their very cut, have a force directed to the right, while others have a force to the left. Many vertical, standing stones have a dominant force and create a solid up-and-down line in the garden. Inclining stones suggest movement to the left or right. As mentioned, stones can be used by themselves, but, when used in groups, the line forces must complement each other; this is accomplished by placement.

### Arranging Stones

Vertical, standing stones give a feeling of height; in groups they convey an excitement and immediately capture the eye. By themselves they present a jarring mood, so give them a background of tall plants, such as bamboo, rather than other rocks that will obscure and create a formless picture. (You can, as a lesser alternative, use a gravel or pebble background.)

Low, horizontal stones, which are more peaceful in mood, should hug the earth and appear as integral parts of the ground. Low stones are stable and look like mounds, and, because they are wider than their height, they seem more peaceful the more massive they are. Their edges should be concealed by moss or ground covers, and vertical stones generally should not be used with them. Low stones are especially attractive near water.

Irregular boulders have strong planes and deep crevices. They are *(above) Here stone unites with slate to create a delightful patio. Only a few plants are used, but they are strategically placed to provide just the right amount of contrast with the stone materials. Photo courtesy of Buckingham-Virginia Slate Company; Taylor, Lewis & Associates, Architects; Norfolk, Virginia.*

*(below) A dry garden using lightweight Featherock; the scene is eye-appealing and requires no maintenance. Photo courtesy of Featherock, Inc.*

used as a counterpoint for other forms, although they don't work with large vertical stones because one distracts from the other. Irregular stones are best used in a group of three, in three different sizes, for a very dramatic arrangement.

Flat stones are valuable as stepping-stones and for balancing low, mound-shaped stones.

### How to Handle Stones

Natural stones are heavy, but this should not stop you from having your quiet garden. With the proper tools, stones can be put in place with less trouble than you think. Mechanical help goes a long way in making stone gardening easy.

Do not try to lift stones with sheer muscle power; it won't work, and you could end up in the hospital! You might be able to lift a fifty-pound or even a hundred-pound stone, but the twisting and pulling necessary to get it in place is far beyond the average person's capacity.

You can, of course, hire garden contractors with power equipment to do the job, but this is usually expensive. With a little muscle power and a steel rod or a hefty piece of lumber, you can move a three-hundred- to four-hundred-pound stone. Use the bar or rod as a lever and inch the stone along. (*Warning:* Do not try this on a downhill grade.)

Perhaps the best inexpensive way to place a large stone is the old-fashioned method of moving it on three or four steel rollers, inching the stone to the desired position. This takes time and patience, so do not hurry it or you will be in trouble. Putting the stone on a piece of board or on a gunnysack or canvas will also work.

For very large stones (and to save yourself a lot of labor), use a block-and-tackle rig with a large tree as an anchor for the block. Tie a protective coating of canvas or gunnysacks around the tree to avoid harming it from the abrasion of the rope. However, the most efficient way to move a stone is with a chain hoist, which can be rented, but be sure you know how to operate it properly.

Installing rocks in the garden is not difficult once they are hauled to their places. The main considerations are that they are firmly placed and look permanent rather than in a precarious position. Before setting the rock in place, dig a depression where it is to sit.

*Large rocks for sale at building supply yard. Note that each rock has a definite character; select ones with most interest for the stone and sand garden. Photo by Joyce R. Wilson.*

*Small stones in various colors are also at suppliers' building yards. Sometimes these are called river-washed stones. Photo by Joyce R. Wilson.*

*These stones are more angular and more contemporary in feeling than the rounded rocks in photo 5. Select with care, for these stones do not blend well with every landscape. Photo by Joyce R. Wilson.*

The depth of the depression varies with the size of the rock, but at least one-third of the rock should be buried so that it seems to be part of the earth, rather than just sitting on top of it.

If a rock is such a shape that you cannot get it deeply anchored in the ground, use small stones underneath and then pack soil between the stones and around them to build a base for the larger stone.

# 2. The Beauty of Sand, Gravel, and Other Materials

You have undoubtedly seen beautiful sand formations at the beach. When sand is combined with strategically placed rock or gravel, a few tufts of grass, or an occasional plant, the resulting landscape is indeed handsome.

However, because of the simplicity of the materials, a sand and gravel garden requires careful design. This garden is perhaps best used in small areas for accent or for an island or seaside effect with raked patterns. Sand and gravel are stark in appearance, so a few plants may be needed for color and warmth.

### Sand

Sand has always been a basic part of many Japanese gardens. It imparts a clean, fresh feeling and does not soil clothing, but it is a difficult material to use effectively. Its beauty lies in its simplicity, which means that you have to use it in the right places, in the right patterns, and with the right accompaniments. Too much sand area is too stark and too simple, and not to everyone's liking.

In entries and at doorways, the "dry garden" of sand is highly effective with a few properly placed rocks. Sand is also used in the garden for dramatic contrast and beauty.

The beauty of sand is that it is a perfect foil for stone groups and

*Sand and gravel are used for this front entranceway, with two stones to accent the composition. Photo by Clint Bryant.*

grass and that it can be raked into appealing patterns. White and blue sands are especially handsome, and some of the umber shades are effective too. Black sand is impressive and can be stunning; brown colors are refined and elegant. Remember that stark white can cause glare in sun.

Do not use beach sand; it will blow away in a strong wind and wash out in rain. Use sand at least one-fourth-inch mesh, so that it will stay in place and be small enough to hold a raked design.

To prepare a sand garden, clear out all weeds and any debris, dig down to about three inches, and excavate the area. Put in the first layer of sand and roll it in place; add more sand on top for the raked design. A simpler and less expensive method is to install a layer of concrete over the excavated site and then add sand. With this plan you do not use as much material and can keep out weeds, although polyethylene sheeting will do that too.

Definitely use a pattern in the sand to alert people not to walk on the area. And with a raked design you can choose your garden at will.

Sand is available from most building supply yards, and more colors are offered now than in previous years.

## Gravel

If you need a broad sweep of pattern, but the area is such that paving is difficult or grass won't grow, consider loose gravel; it is easy to work with and inexpensive. Whether the garden is informal or formal, the addition of a gravel arch or sweep as an accent adds beauty to the overall plan. The color and texture bring a dimension to the garden that is, in most cases, highly desirable. However, the area should not be used for excessive foot traffic.

Gravel has a neat and trim appearance that will highlight any area. It is easy to work with in tight corners or in awkward places, and it is the only material that you can actually mold with your hands. The idea may not seem practical at first, since every year gravel must be replaced, but gravel can be easily applied by even the novice and can, if handled properly, be very handsome.

### Grades of Gravel

Natural river-washed gravel, round and gray or chocolate colored, can be used in varying ways to highlight the garden. It is commonly available by the size of the diameter of the stone: ¼, ⅜, ⅝, ⅞, 1½, and 2¼ inches. To cover 150 square feet to a depth of two inches, you will need about one cubic yard of gravel. A truckload is usually three to five cubic yards. Occasionally, gravel is offered in hundred-pound sacks.

Do not use too lightweight a grade; it will float away in the rain. Select, at a minimum, ¼-inch gravel.

To make a gravel area, dig out two to three inches of soil and smooth and tamp down the earth. Add gravel to fill the desired pattern, and roll it in place (with a rented roller) so that it is packed down. If you do not want weeds to sprout, after digging out the foundation add a sheet of polyethylene plastic; then set the gravel in place.

### Cobble

Cobble is round-edged, large gravel, 1 to 6 inches in diameter. At one time cobbles were difficult to find, but now they are readily available at most building suppliers. Most cobbles are from Mexico, and they come in several shades of gray as well as black and white.

*Gravel and crushed stone come in many sizes; use depends on their application; whether for paths or accent areas. Photos by Joyce R. Wilson.*

Because cobbles are difficult to walk on, they should be used sparingly in areas of foot traffic, although they do provide handsome texture in awkward places around an area or as inserts in concrete patios. And don't forget that wherever there are cobble areas there is no maintenance.

Installing cobbles is simple: press them on end or flat in a wet concrete base. Put them far enough into the concrete so that they are firmly in place, or later they may come loose. Be sure that the cobbles are packed closely together and that as little as possible of the mortar shows. Let the stones harden for about ten days. Then clean them with a 10 percent solution of muriatic acid to remove excess mortar and to bring out the color of the stones.

Cobbles can be laid in beautiful swirled, curved, or geometric patterns. Coursed patterns are cobbles laid in more or less single rows; other cobbles can be randomly placed or laid parallel. Each pattern has a distinctive character and should be used in an appropriate place. For example, around a tree-well of not more than ten feet in diameter, six-inch-diameter black or gray cobbles, uniformly sized and laid in a circular pattern, are stunning. In a garden corner a random pattern is highly effective, and for edging driveways parallel patterns are fine.

Cobbles can also be used as fill material; install loose cobbles in a plant area surrounded by a brick edging. With the addition of a few well-placed plants this becomes a decorative, no-care garden area. Be sure to use cobbles of uniform size, for therein lies the beauty of this type of stone gardening.

You can get a variation of aggregate paving by using cobbles as a seeded surface in a bed of concrete. Install the concrete. Lay cobbles over the surface and press them into place with a wood float, so that the concrete comes to the surface. Let the mixture set a few hours. Brush away loose mortar while the concrete is still somewhat crumbly, taking care not to dislodge the cobbles. Then alternately brush and hose with a fine spray.

### Crushed Stone

Crushed stone is made from larger rocks and has sharp edges and points. (Do not confuse it with gravel, which is rounded by the action of sea and stream.) The crushed material is available in gray tones

*Large cobbles have many uses in the stone and sand garden; these are not uniform in size, but Mexican cobbles are and come in gray or black. Photo by Joyce R. Wilson.*

*Uniform-sized cobbles create a false water garden in this landscape. Photo by author.*

*Cobbles in a handsome pattern frame a water fountain and add necessary eye interest to the scene. Photo by Clint Bryant.*

in diameters of ⅜, ½, ¾, or 1½ inches, but in place it is not as attractive as natural gravel. Crushed stone is difficult to walk on and is not a permanent landscaping material. It is used because of its low cost and easy application.

Best confined to limited areas, crushed stones can be used as a frame for a large rock, as an accent in an awkward corner where a plant would not grow, or as a path. Once introduced into the garden, repeat crushed stone elsewhere in the area to balance the composition.

Crushed stone of rust color recently has been available at suppliers; this is a form of Lavarock and is colorful and attractive when used in small areas.

### Other Materials

Marble, an elegant material, is available in black, white, or gray chips about ½ inch in diameter. It can be effectively used in a landscape with large rocks and picturesque trees and shrubs. The material shines in the rain and offers drama. Although marble chips are frequently part of dish gardens and trayscapes, their cost usually prohibits large installations.

For a small oriental garden off a bedroom or bathroom I highly recommend marble chips, because they have flair and elegance and they impart a serene quality to the garden picture. Installation of marble chips is the same as of gravel, although a stronger hosing is necessary.

Fir bark is a versatile product being used more and more in contemporary gardens. It is an inexpensive and highly effective material for borders, coverings, mulching, and decorative effect. It is the bark of the Douglas fir tree, steamed and broken into variously sized pellets. It is available in pea and pebble size and in chunks from one to three inches in diameter and is sold in convenient sacks or by the yard from local building dealers.

Fir bark deteriorates slowly, does not wash away in the rain, and blends well with most outdoor plants and accessories. Like gravel, it is easy to put in place. (My small garden of evergreens is framed with fir bark in a sweeping arc to accent the trees. I have to replace the bark about every eighteen months, but this is hardly costly in view of its advantages.) Weeding is rarely necessary, and even in very large areas fir bark looks attractive. You can use it with practically

*Fir bark, a natural material, looks good in the garden. Here it is used to outline a tree-round path.* Photo by author.

any type of plant—grasses, shrubs, ground cover, trees—without fear of distracting from the total scene.

Install fir bark in sweeping arcs and curves rather than in solid geometric patterns; the material looks highly attractive when used in this manner. Dig down about three inches, firm the soil, and lay a sheet of black plastic over the ground. Add two to three inches of bark. Your only maintenance will be removing twigs or leaves that fall from overhead trees.

# 3. Planning the Stone and Sand Garden

Careful planning and design are essential in the stone and sand garden, for its beauty depends on simplicity—a few plants and some well placed rocks. There is little room for error here. In the traditional garden mistakes can often be camouflaged. And too, where there are many plants, one not appropriate for the landscape can be hidden by others.

Graceful branches of tree and shrub, foliage, and texture are used to achieve an ideal landscape. And color is the catalyst that makes the garden an eye-appealing experience. There should be no abrupt color changes to ruin the peaceful character of the scene. Grays and greens of leaves and limb and the earthy colors of brown and black rocks are our palette. An occasional dramatic statement with dark flowers is permissible too.

Above all, avoid clutter and practice restraint; relate the house and garden into one. Use texture and form; concentrate on small details to delight the eye and stimulate the senses.

*This entrance is well planned, the geometric design handsome and ideal for the stone and gravel application. Photo by Clint Bryant.*

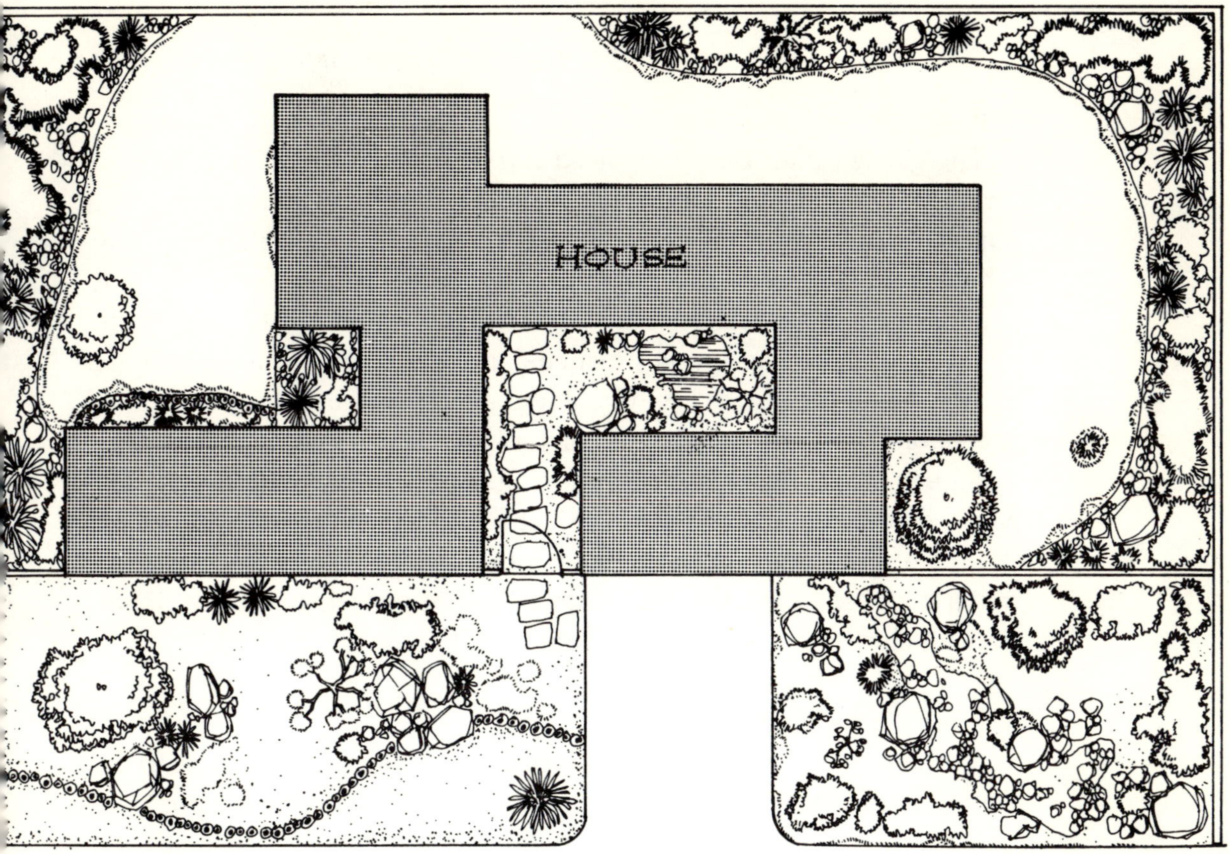

## PLAN

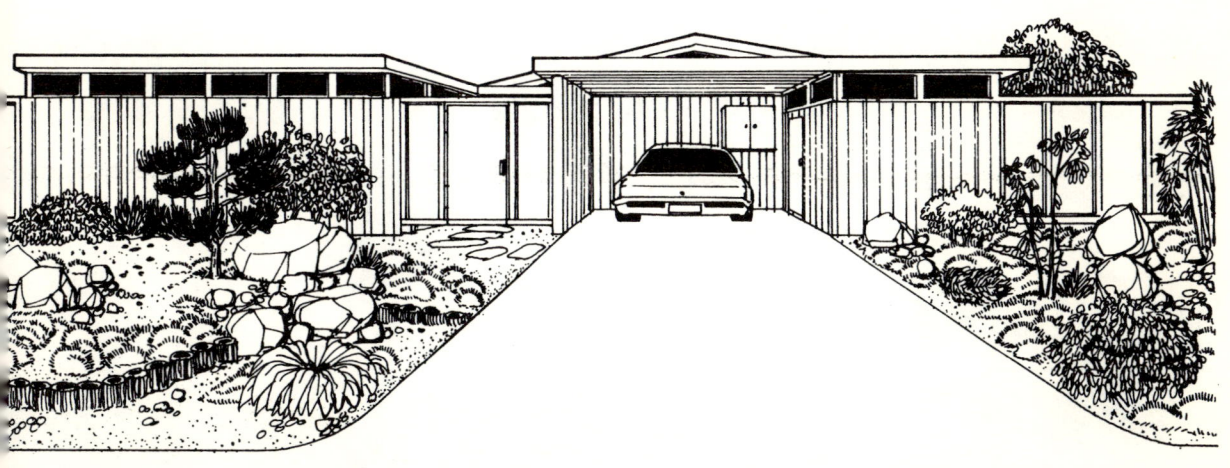

## SAND AND STONE GARDEN

### Planning on Paper

The garden plan on paper need not be exact; it can be a sketch. Draw in boundary lines and existing plant material. Then place tissue paper over the original sheet of paper, and start the plan showing where the rocks, trees, and gravel areas will be located. Use a different shape for each, and remember to put in walks and points of interest.

When the final design is finished—and make several until you are satisfied—color the areas (with colored pencils) where there are grass, gravel, and stones. A definite color match is not necessary; simply use green for grass, white for gravel, and brown or black for stones. Make certain you are pleased with the color harmony as well as the design of the garden. Next, on another sheet of paper, mark the materials needed for the plan: rocks, stone, gravel, plants; estimate how much stone you need. (See chapter 2.)

### The Garden Design

As mentioned, strive for simplicity and use plant materials as tools: evergreens for stability and year-round effect, spring-flowering trees for splashes of color, and autumn foliage for the fall scene. If you have selected materials intelligently, in winter the garden will stand on its own merit.

*Shaped trees highlight this yard; a few stones create the necessary balance in the landscape. Photo by author.*

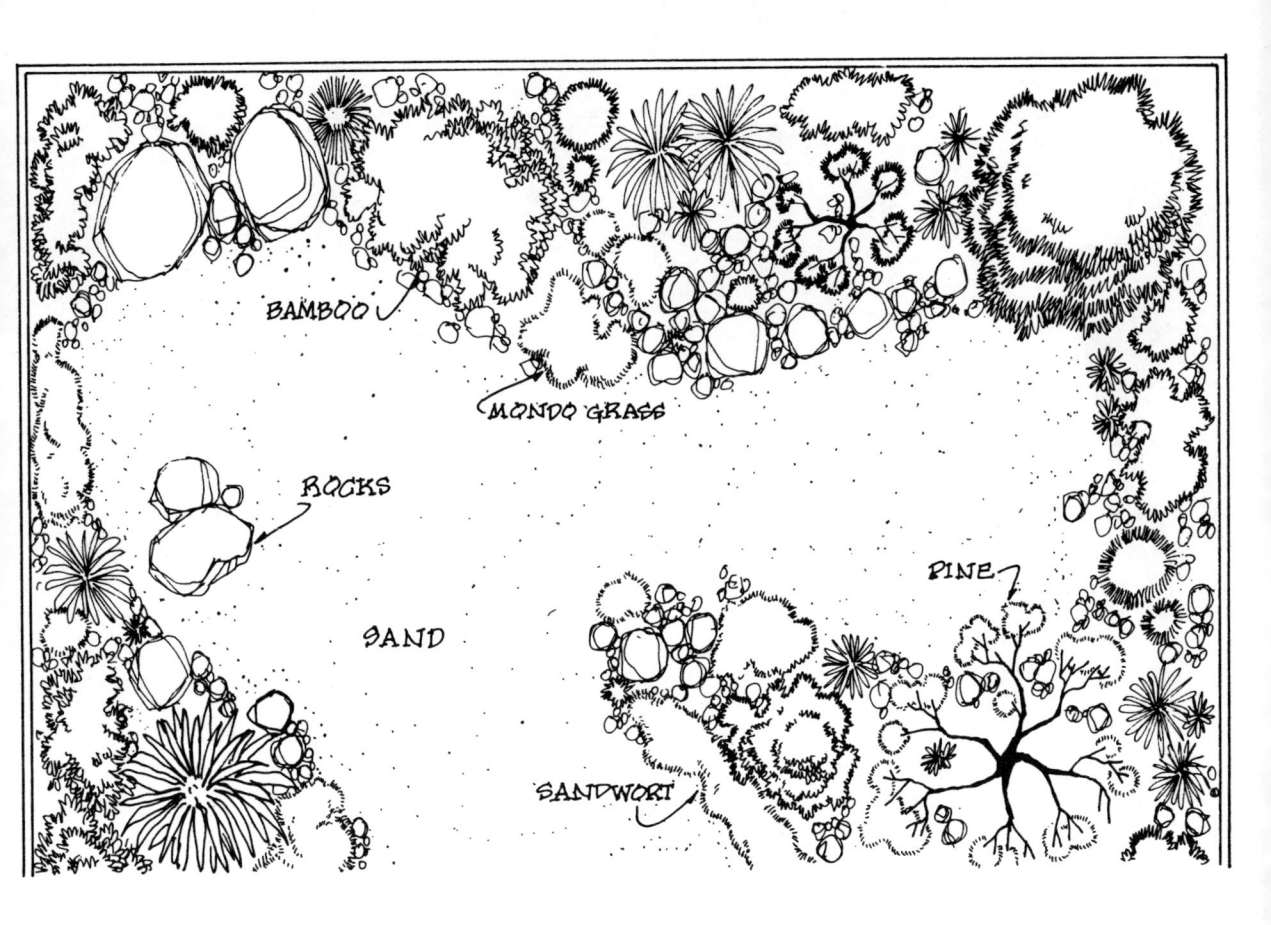

# SAND AND STONE GARDEN

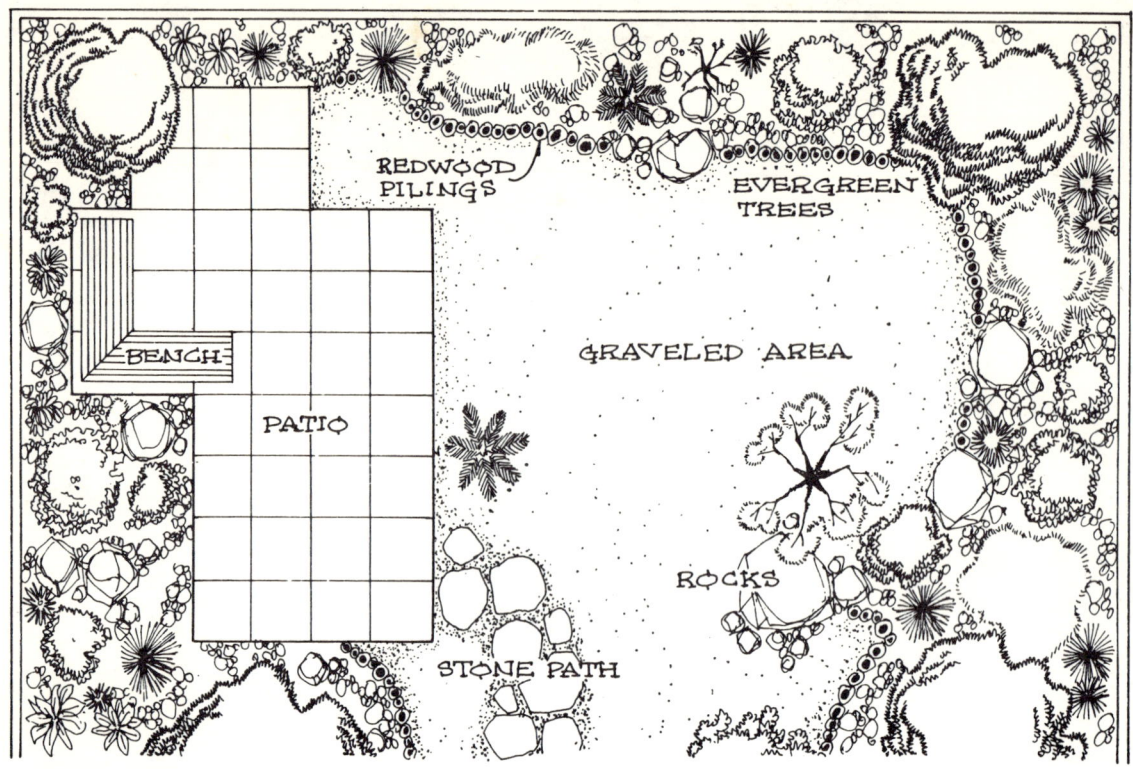

**PLAN**

**GARDEN**

# STONE AND SAND GARDEN

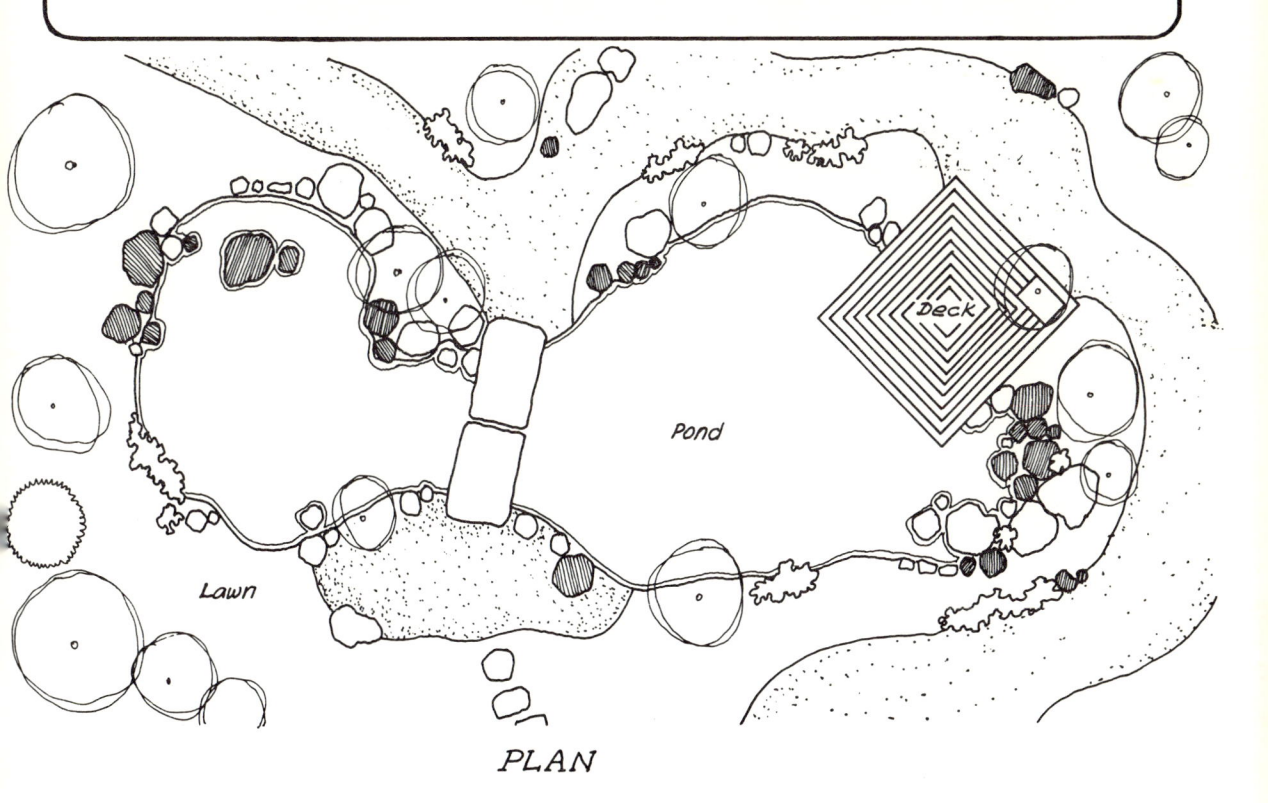

PLAN

Lawn

Pond

Deck

The size and the shape of the property determine what kind of garden to have. Absolute landscaping rules cannot be given, for each site is different. However, good design principles—balance, proportion, and unity—are universal.

For proper balance in the garden leave space between plantings and rock groups, so that each element has dimension and form. Use vertical and horizontal accents carefully to achieve good balance. Proportion relates to the parts of the garden, their symmetry, and their relationships. Each plant, each rock must be in scale with its counterparts. All parts of the garden must relate to achieve the final principle of good design—unity. Try to join the plantings with the rocks, gravel, or sand so that they create a total composition. This is done by repetition of a pattern, a material, a texture, or a color. This is the thread that unifies and ties the garden elements into a pleasing design.

Although most gardens are at the rear of the property, stone and sand landscapes are also effective as a front or entry court (indeed, this peaceful scene is highly desirable to introduce a guest to the home) or as a side garden, which is generally long and narrow. Stone and sand materials establish an intimacy that is often lacking in the traditional flower garden.

The city garden is another landscape well suited to stone and sand gardening. You do not need to worry about pollution harming plants, about tons of soil, or about frequent replenishing. A few plants only require a few sacks of soil, and the plants are easily replaced if they do not succeed under city conditions. Gravel areas and interesting rock groups require no soil. Further, if there is little sun, this garden of a few plants survives while other gardens, heavily planted, might perish (or at best be a constant struggle to maintain).

In many large Japanese city situations you find intimate stone and sand gardens and for valid reasons. Care is at a minimum once the garden is established.

Making It Work

Gardens that are installed without thought to basic needs will always be a burden. Certain fundamentals, such as underground lines, water, and drainage, should be attended to first. If you had a dependable contractor, leveling, grading, and proper drainage of

*A beautifully designed sideyard using patterned cobbles and low plants. Roses provide the backdrop. Photo by Clint Bryant.*

*Gravel, stone, and a few plants are the materials used in this garden plan. Photo by Clint Bryant.*

water will be satisfactory. Check to be sure that there is ample water runoff into proper drain sewers.

If the basic needs of the garden are satisfactory, it is time to start the earth work. Decide now if there is to be a patio and where you want mounds of soil for eye interest. Fill in low areas where water might accumulate, and remedy hilly situations that are unsightly. Then it is time to install paths and steps—not later when the garden is completed. Next, start to put the rocks and stones into place. Know where they will go (refer to your paper plan), so that you will not have to move materials around needlessly. Once the rock and gravel groupings are in place, select trees, shrubs, and ground covers. Install only a few plants at first; see how they appear in the garden before you proceed with other plant material.

I have purposely left major structures, such as garden arbors and fences, for last. While it is nice to have the property enclosed while you work on it, materials must be delivered and transported to their proper places. If you have fenced yourself in, getting the materials to the site will be impossible. Gravel and stone are delivered tailgate (to your doorstep). There must be some access for trucks to get to the site and the closer the material can be dumped to where it belongs, the easier it will be for you. It saves time and money.

Finally, add accessories, such as stone urns, containers, lanterns, and basins, after all construction and planting have been done. Only the finished design will suggest what kind of accessories to use.

# 4. Plants for Stone and Sand Gardening

Although some stone and sand gardens are without vegetation, most gardens do rely on some plant material for an overall attractive picture. But the plants in this garden are used in a different way from those in the traditional garden. They must be individually selected,

*Trees, shrubs, and flowers are a natural trio in this handsome scene. The three areas of rock are perfectly chosen for shape and contrast. Photo by Molly Adams.*

*A few flowers and a few rocks—and a garden corner becomes appealing. Photo by Clint Bryant.*

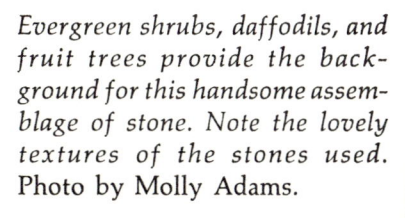

*Evergreen shrubs, daffodils, and fruit trees provide the background for this handsome assemblage of stone. Note the lovely textures of the stones used. Photo by Molly Adams.*

meticulously placed, and properly trained and pruned to be in character with the garden. The stone and sand garden by nature suggests a graceful place of repose, so plants must be picturesque and in union with the scene.

Perhaps the greatest difference between plants in this garden and the traditional one is that here plants are given space; there are rarely masses of bloom or foliage, but, rather, carefully selected groups.

### Plant Material

Don't think about plants until the stones are in place, for in the stone arrangement you will find clues as to what kind of plants to select. Trees are always a good starting point; they are permanent in feeling and establish a reference point. Shrubs can be used to a lesser, but still effective, degree; however, flowering plants should be used sparingly, if at all. The garden depends on rocks and stones, with plants as additional helpers rather than as the attraction.

All kinds of plants, such as pines and azaleas, can be in the garden, but some are more effective than others. Deciduous trees, such as birch, gingko, Japanese maple, and willow, are all possibilities. Evergreen trees offer a larger choice: spruce, cedar, juniper, cryptomeria, and chamaecyparis. Shrubs can be represented by abelia, aralia, barberry, bayberry, elaeagnus, euonymus, fatsia, holly, Japanese privet, rhododendron, and podocarpus. For flowering plants, select anemone, camellia, chrysanthemum, gentian, hydrangea, peony, daffodil, and crocus. Not to be forgotten are the wonderful flowering fruit trees.

When putting plants in place, allow enough space around them. Don't set them at random; group several plants that are related in texture and form, but are different in height. Use vertical accent as well as horizontal points.

Do not put too many kinds of plants in the garden. It is better to use a lot of one variety rather than many kinds of plants. A single specimen with gnarled branches or picturesque growth is often a master stroke. By itself it can make more of a statement than a group of plants.

Try to locate plants at different levels rather than in one flat plane. Raised or sunken plantings offer drama and visual interest while providing dimension. Combine plants the way they would grow in

*Fruit trees are always handsome in bloom, add color and dimension in the garden. Photo by Clint Bryant; courtesy of Armstrong Nurseries.*

*Flowering cherry trees are popular in stone and sand gardens. This is Prunus Hally Jolivette, a handsome tree. Photo courtesy of Wayside Garden.*

*Close-up of flowers of Prunus Hally Jolivette. Photo courtesy of Wayside Garden.*

*Crabapples, with their picturesque form, are always appealing in the garden. Photo courtesy of Wayside Garden.*

nature; for example, don't mix plants from woodlands with desert plants.

Keep plants in scale to the garden by pruning them regularly. Use shrubs for their sculptured branches, not just for bloom. Finally, once again, use flowering plants with discretion. Too much color is distracting when viewed against stones and rocks. It is often shocking, for the stone and sand garden relies on textures and muted colors.

CARE OF PLANTS

For all plants use a well-prepared soil with adequate nutrients. If the subsoil is hard, break it up and add organic matter, such as ground bark, peat moss, or leaf mold. When planting trees, dig deep holes to accommodate roots, and water plants heavily the first few months until they are established. For balled or container-grown trees, use planting holes about twice as wide and one-and-a-half times as deep as the root ball. Set the plants on a cushion of soil and add new soil. Soak well, filling the basin two or three times as you go along.

Pruning and training are the keys to success with trees in the stone and sand garden. To have well-shaped trees, start cutting them back and shaping them when they are young and continue to do so yearly. Even drastic pruning, if properly done when necessary, will not harm a tree.

To train trees, remove dead, weak, and crossing branches, thin remaining branches, and decide on the pattern you want to set. (You can select disc, pompon, tier, or elliptical shapes; all call for drastic pruning of the limbs and foliage.) Train tree branches by pulling them down to form a graceful arch, but be careful not to break the branches by using too much weight. Anchor them with stones, or wire the branches to stakes in the ground. Keep top growth pinched back, and emphasize horizontal branching patterns rather than vertical ones. Once the main trunk and supporting branches are established, maintain the basic form so that the tree never gets out of scale.

Shrubs should be treated like trees: that is, pruned and trained in low mounds and round contours (especially azaleas immediately after they bloom), to provide contrasts in color, texture, and mass.

If you use flowers, avoid large mass arrangements or long border accents. Use one type of flower as just a stroke of color in the garden;

*Close-up of crabapple blossoms. Photo courtesy of Wayside Garden.*

*Favorite flowers of oriental gardens are chrysanthemums, well known and always colorful. Photo courtesy of Wayside Garden.*

*Anemones come in lusty dark colors and make perfect contrasts in the stone and sand landscape. Photo courtesy of Wayside Garden.*

try to avoid pastel shades. Rely on bright colors, such as purple and red, for contrast and drama.

How to Use Plants

Too many plants should not be used in the stone and sand garden, and those that are must be placed properly. Here are some helpful hints:

1. Use deciduous trees with autumn color close to the house or against a fence or evergreen background.
2. When working with coniferous evergreens, such as spruce, fir, and pine, place them as a background or use them in the garden to show form. With pines, plant single trees to emphasize the sculptural growth.
3. Flowering trees, like plum, peach, or cherry, are especially lovely and need a dark background to show them off effectively.
4. Large trees, such as gingko, oak, and maple, should be placed near the base of a hill or to one side so that branches will overhang the mound.
5. Be sure to prune junipers to display basic forms and shapes.
6. For bold effects use large-leaved plants, such as podocarpus and aralia.
7. Use azaleas and rhododendrons in mass to cover a hill, and use hedges and grasses near water areas.

The following lists of shrubs, trees, and flowering plants are good choices for your stone and sand gardens. I have, of course, not included all possibilities; you can experiment and discover for yourself the enjoyment of designing your own garden. Check with local nurseryman for hardiness of plants in your area.

List of Shrubs

*Abelia grandiflora* (glossy abelia). Evergreen to partially deciduous. Grows to eight feet or more. Flowers white or pink tinged.
*A. grandiflora* 'Prostrata.' Smaller and low growing.
*Aralia elata* (Japanese angelica tree). Narrow-toothed leaflets; bold leaved. Can grow tall. Frequently multistemmed.
*Ardisia crispa.* Clusters of red berries in autumn.

**tiered**

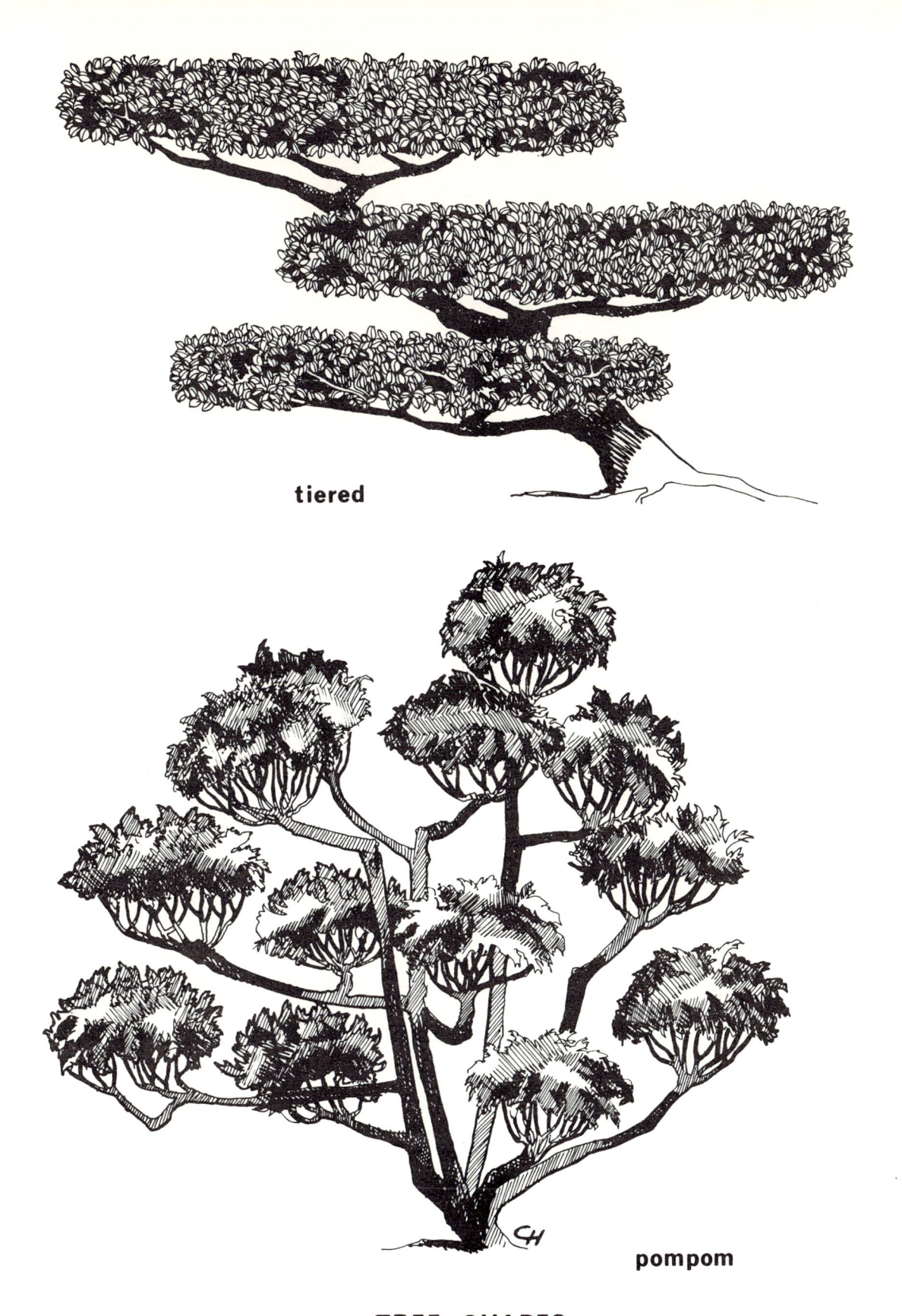

**pompom**

**TREE SHAPES**

*Aspidistra elatior* (cast-iron plant). Lush green foliage accent.

*Aucuba japonica* (Japanese aucuba). A good shrub for shade; easily trained. Dark green, shiny leaves with toothed edges. Grows to about ten feet.

Azalea. (See chapter 6.)

*Berberis buxifolia* (Magellan barberry). Grows upright to six feet. Small leathery leaves.

*B. mentorensis.* Compact grower to seven feet. Leaves dark green. Easy to train.

*B. thunbergii* (Japanese barberry). Graceful grower with slender arching branches to six feet. Densely foliaged with deep green leaves turning red in fall. Useful shrub. (Red-leafed dwarf variety also available.)

*Buxus microphylla japonica* (Japanese boxwood). Lovely compact foliage, bright green in summer and bronze in winter. Grows to six feet. Easily shaped.

*B. m. koreana* (Korean boxwood). Slower and lower growing.

*Camellia japonica.* Variable in size, growth rate, and habit. Innumerable varieties in varied flower forms from two to five inches in diameter.

*C. sasanqua.* Lovely foliage; pretty flowers. Hundreds of varieties.

*Daphne cneorum* (garland daphne). Spreading plant with trailing branches covered with narrow leaves.

*Elaeagnus angustifolia* (Russian olive). Really a tree, but can be clipped and trained as a hedge. Angular trunk; branches with silver gray leaves.

*Euonymus fortunei.* Good broad-leaved evergreen shrub with dark, rich green leaves with toothed edges. Many varieties.

*Fatsia japonica* (Japanese aralia). Big, glossy, dark green leaves, deeply lobed. Grows to eight feet. Can be thinned to show branch structure.

*Gardenia florida.* Fragrant single white blossoms in summer.

*Hydrangea macrophylla* (bigleaf or garden hydrangea). Deciduous big-leaved shrub with large clusters of long-lasting flowers.

*Ilex crenata* (Japanese holly). Dense and erect with finely toothed leaves.

*Juniperus chinensis* (Chinese juniper, shrub type). Many varieties

pyramidal					disc

**TREE SHAPES**

Dwarf Nectarine

Dwarf Plum 'Satsuma'

and many sizes, most with dark green or blue green needles.

*J. c. 'Pfitzeriana'* (Pfitzer juniper). A large group with many varieties useful in the stone and sand garden.

*J. procumbens* (Japanese garden juniper). Grows to three feet. Feathery blue green foliage and spreading branches.

*J. p. 'Nana.'* Grows to twelve inches; slow-growing and dense. Blue gray foliage.

*Ligustrum japonicum* (Japanese privet). Dense, compact grower to ten feet. Roundish oval leaves. Good for shaping.

*Myrica pennsylvanica* (bayberry). Dense compact grower to ten feet. Glossy green foliage.

*Nerium oleander.* A basic shrub that seems to grow in all conditions. Most varieties reach eight to twelve feet. Narrow leaves and clusters of flowers in white, yellow, pink, salmon, and red.

*Osmanthus fragrans* (sweet olive). Easily trained. Glossy green leaves and white inconspicuous flowers.

*Paeonia moutan* (peony). Spectacular treelike plant with large flowers and lush foliage.

*Photinia glabra* (Japanese photinia). Broad, dense growth to ten feet. Red leaves in winter.

*P. serrulata* (Chinese photinia). Crisp, deep green leaves. Can grow to twenty-five feet.

*Pieris japonica* (lily-of-the-valley shrub). Dense, tiered grower to ten feet. Glossy, dark green leaves. (Sometimes called Andromeda.)

*Pittosporum tobira.* Dense shrub (sometimes tree) to fifteen feet. Leathery leaves and dense growth. White flowers in early spring.

*Raphiolepis indica* (India hawthorn). Grows to five feet. Handsome leaves and flowers.

*R. umbellata.* Round, leathery, dark green leaves; white blooms. Grows to six feet.

Rhododendron. (See chapter 6.)

Rose. (See "Flowering Plants," this chapter.)

*Sambucus racemosa* (red elderberry). Bush grows to six feet. Toothed leaves and white flowers.

*Spiraea thunbergii.* Showy, billowy plant to five feet. Arching branches and small white flowers.

*Viburnum dilatatum* (linden viburnum). Broad and compact to ten

**heavy garden stakes**

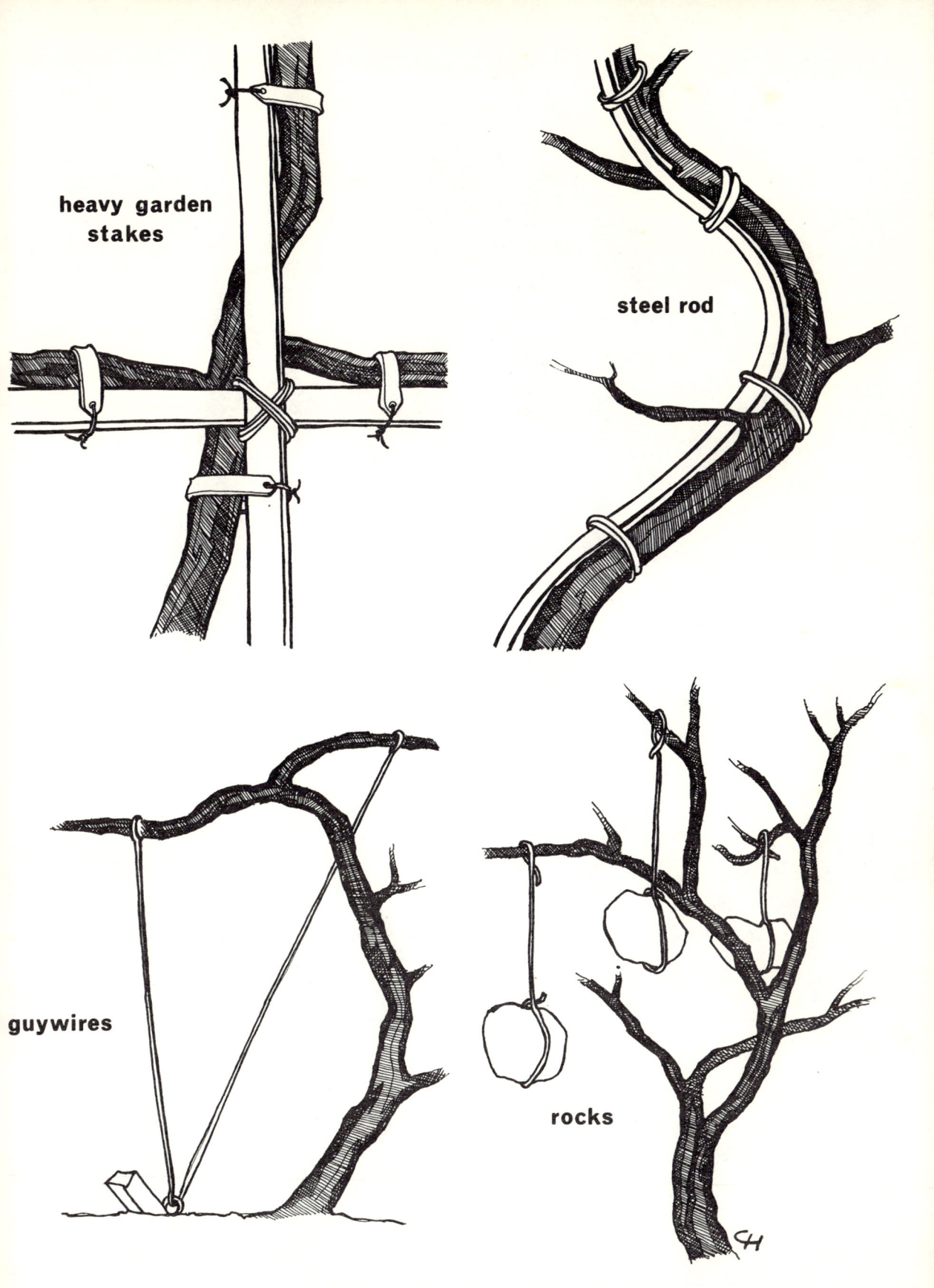

**steel rod**

**guywires**

**rocks**

**DEVICES FOR SHAPING TREES**

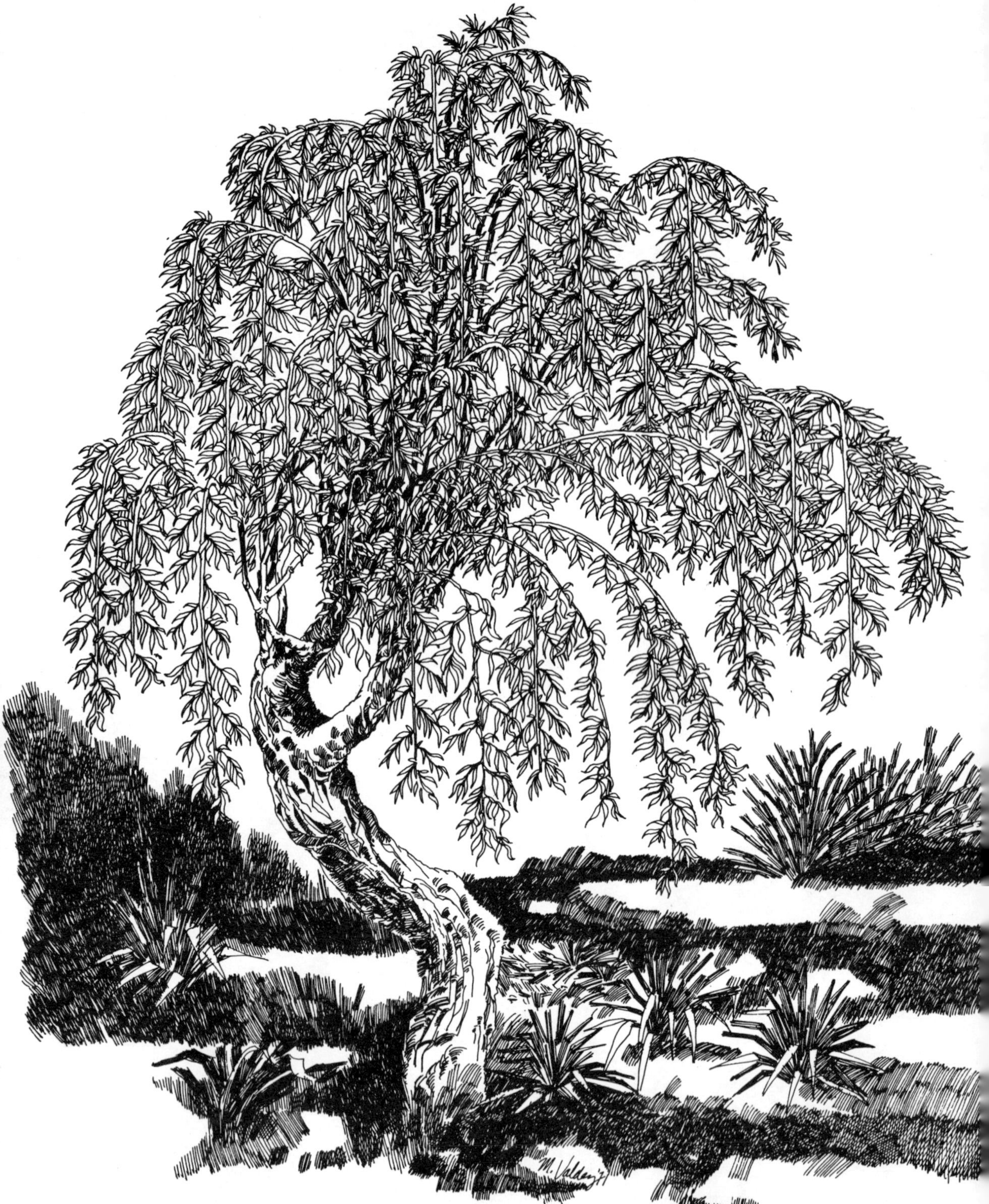

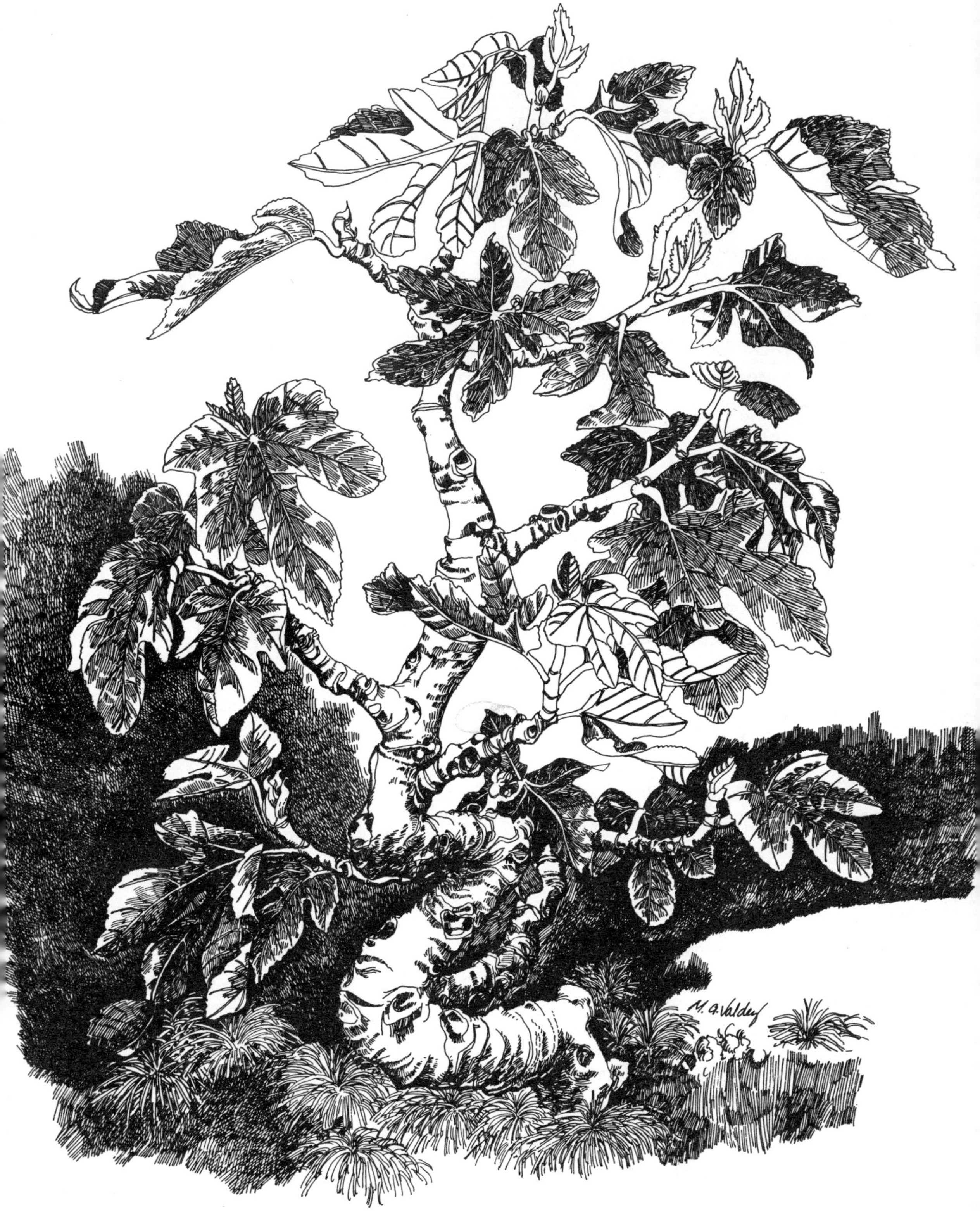

feet. Gray green round leaves and tiny, creamy white flowers.

*Wisteria floribunda* (Japanese wisteria). Twining, woody vine of incredible beauty in bloom; long clusters of violet to violet blue flowers.

## List of Trees

*Acer buergerianum* (trident maple). Low-spreading tree to twenty feet. Glossy green leaves; red in fall.

*A. ginnala* (amur maple). Can be grown as a multitrunked tree to about twenty-five feet. Striking fall color.

*A. japonicum* (fullmoon maple). Small, slow-growing tree best known by its two varieties:

*A. j.* 'Aconitifolium' (fernleaf fullmoon maple). Fine fall color.

*A. j.* 'Aureum' (golden fullmoon maple). Pale gold leaves in spring; pale chartreuse all summer.

*A. palmatum* (Japanese maple). A multi stemmed tree, both delicate and graceful; year-round beauty.

*A. p.* 'Atropurpureum' (red Japanese maple). Brilliant color.

*A. p.* 'Burgundy Lace.' Deeply lobed leaves.

*A. p.* 'Dissectum' (laceleaf Japanese maple). Almost threadlike leaves.

*A. p.* 'Ornatum' (red laceleaf Japanese maple). Bright red leaves.

*Aesculus carnea* (red horse chestnut). A round-headed tree to forty feet. Large, dark green leaves and pink to red blooms.

*Albizzia julibrissin* (silk tree). Lovely, graceful tree to forty feet. Pink fluffy flowers.

*Betula verrucosa* (*B. alba* or *B. pendula*; European white birch). Delicate and lacy; upright branching with weeping side branches. Can grow to forty feet. Rich green, glossy foliage.

*B. v.* 'Dalecarlica' ('Laciniata'; cutleaf weeping birch). Very pendant growth and deeply cut leaves.

*B. v.* 'Fastigiata' (pyramidal white birch). Upright habit.

*Cedrus deodara* (Deodar cedar). The true cedar; grows to eighty feet. Tall, fast growing, but can be kept in bounds by pruning.

*Cercis chinensis* (Chinese redbud). Open tree to ten feet. Clusters of magnificent, deep rose blooms.

## Plants for Stone and Sand Gardening

Chamaecyparis. (See chapters 5 and 6.)

*Cinnamomum camphora* (camphor tree). Heavy spreading limbs. Grows to fifty feet. New foliage is bronzy; good winter color. Outstanding.

*Cornus kousa* (Kousa dogwood). Multistemmed to twenty feet. Dense horizontal growth habit. Yellow and scarlet fall color.

*Crataegus oxyacantha* 'Paul's Scarlet.' Handsome tree to fifteen feet. Deep edged leaves and rose to red flowers.

*C. phaenopyrum* (Washington hawthorn). Light and open limb structure. Grows to twenty-five feet.

*Cryptomeria japonica* (Japanese cedar). A graceful evergreen with pendulous branches.

*C. j.* 'Elegans' (plume cedar). Feathery, grayish green foliage; coppery red in winter. Easily pruned.

*C. j.* 'Lobbii Nana.' Upright dwarf to three feet. Dark green foliage.

*Diospyros kaki* (oriental persimmon). Squatty, but sculptural with wide, spreading branches. Scarlet color in winter.

*Ficus retusa* (Indian laurel fig). Grows to twenty-five feet. Long leaves; ornamental.

*Gingko biloba.* Graceful, robust tree. Can grow to thirty-five feet. Gold color in fall.

*Juniperus chinensis* (Chinese juniper). Grows to twenty-five feet. Blue green foliage. Usually offered as *J. chinensis* 'Columnaris.'

*J. scopulorum* 'Pendula.' Grows to twenty feet. Silvery foliage and weeping branches.

*Larix leptolepis* (Japanese larch). Can grow to sixty feet. Horizontal branches and drooping habit. Good color year-round.

*Magnolia denudata* (Yulan magnolia). Grows to thirty-five feet. Spectacular flowers; irregular in shape.

*M. kobus.* A sturdy tree; grows to thirty feet. Fine white blossoms.

*M. k. stellata* (star magnolia). Delicate, slow-growing tree. Star-shaped white blossoms.

*Malus floribunda* (Japanese flowering crabapple). Rounded, densely branched tree.

Pinus. (See chapter 6.)

*Salix babylonica* (weeping willow). Popular weeping tree. Grows to forty feet.

*S. matsudana* (Hankow willow). Pyramidal growth to forty feet. Narrow, bright green leaves.

*S. m.* 'Tortuosa' (twisted Hankow willow). Gnarled upright growth to thirty feet. Good sculptural tree.

*Sophora japonica* (Japanese pagoda tree). A good spreading tree to forty feet.

Also suitable are Abies (fir), Alnus (alder), Picea (spruce), Quercus (oak), and Tsuga (hemlock).

### Flowering Fruit Trees

Ornamental fruit trees are valued for their sculptural growth and graceful character. Many are small, some medium-sized; several are evergreen and used for structural purposes, but the majority are the popular deciduous varieties. These are the fine trees that put on such a spectacular spring flower show. They are closely related to the stone fruit group Prunus—apricot, peach, nectarine.

For the stone and sand garden the flowering almond, flowering cherry, and flowering plum tree are popular.

### Cherry

There are many varieties called flowering cherry, and the smaller forms are almost a necessity in the stone and sand garden. The trees need a fast-draining porous soil. They can be pruned when in bloom; remove ungainly branches to force branching.

*Prunus serrulata* (Japanese flowering cherry).
Known through its many cultivated varieties:

*P. s.* 'Beni Hoshi.' Vivid pink flowers and arching, spreading branches.

*P. s.* 'Fugenzo.' Broad, spreading tree. Grows to twenty-five feet.

*P. s.* 'Ojochin.' Compact growth to thirty feet.

*P. s.* 'Shogetsu.' Arching branches; pale pink flowers.

*P. subhirtella autumnalis.* White or pinkish white double flowers in autumn and early spring. Grows to thirty feet.

*P. s.* 'Hally Jolivette.' Grows to eight feet. Double white flowers; pink buds.

*Plants for Stone and Sand Gardening* 45

P. s. pendula (single weeping cherry). Small pink flowers and graceful hanging branches.

P. s. 'Yae-shidare-higan' (double weeping cherry). Rose pink double flowers.

P. *yedoensis* (Yoshino flowering cherry). Graceful, open pattern. Pink to white flowers. Can grow to forty feet.

PLUM

Delightful picturesque trees with pink to rose or white flowers. Frequently used, these trees offer fine color, sculptural and generally easy growth.

*Prunus blireiana.* Grows to twenty-five feet. Reddish purple leaves; green bronze in summer. Pink to rose blooms.

P. *cerasifera* (cherry plum). Pure white flowers; small red plums.

P. *c.* 'Atropurpurea' (purple-leaf plum). Grows to thirty feet.

P. *glandulosa* (dwarf flowering almond). Multibranched; spreading growth to six feet. Double flowers.

P. *mume* (Japanese flowering plum). The longest lived of the flowering fruit trees. Develops into a graceful, gnarled, twenty-foot tree. Several varieties available.

P. *triloba* (flowering almond). Broad leaves and double pink flowers.

Dwarf flowering peach and nectarine trees are also useful in the stone and sand garden; small citrus—orange, lemon, and lime—are still other possibilities.

FLOWERING PLANTS

Anemone. Anemones are a family of lovely plants varying in size from alpine rock-garden types to Japanese varieties. Flowers—all are handsome—appear in spring and extend through fall, depending on the species. Grow plants in well-drained rich soil with some sun. Recommended are *Anemone blanda* (sapphire anemone), with sky-blue blooms; *A. coronaria* (poppy-flowered anemone), with red, blue, or white large flowers; and *A. fulgens* (scarlet windflower), with brilliant red blooms.

Aster. Asters are a large group of perennials ranging from small alpine types to large branching plants. Peak bloom for most asters is summer and fall, with only a few hybrids blooming in spring. Flowers are mainly in shades of blue, red, or purple. Grow plants in full sun with regular watering; they tolerate most soils. Recommended are *Aster alpinus* (rock aster) and *A. frikartii*. *A. novae-angliae* (New England aster) is also handsome.

Campanula. Campanulas are mostly perennial plants, although some are biennials and a few are annuals. Known as bellflowers, these plants include creeping and tufted miniatures, trailers, and erect growers to five feet. Flowers are usually bell-shaped, but occasionally may be star-shaped. Their predominant color is blue. Plants need a sunny moist place. Some bloom in spring and summer; others bloom in fall. Recommended are *Campanula carpatica* (tussock bellflower), with blue or white flowers; *C. elatines garganica*, bearing star-shaped violet blue blooms; and *C. rotundifolia* (bluebell of Scotland), in bright blue.

Chrysanthemum. Chrysanthemum annuals and perennials are predominantly native to China and Japan, where they have been favorite flowers for centuries. The plants need a rich well-drained soil and plenty of sun to be at their best. Recommended are *Chrysanthemum coccineum* (painted daisy), with pink, red, or white flowers; *C. frutescens* (Marguerite), bearing daisylike flowers in a wide range of colors; and *C. maximum* (shasta daisy), white color. *C. morifolium* (florists' chrysanthemum) is available in many flower forms—spoon, cushion, pompon.

Dianthus. Over three hundred species and a large number of varieties make up the Dianthus group. The plants bear single or double flowers in shades of pink, rose, red, orange, and yellow and bloom in spring or summer. Grow plants in light fast-draining soil and sun. Avoid overwatering and shear off faded blooms. Recommended are *Dianthus barbatus* (sweet William), *D. chinensis* (Chinese pink), and *D. deltoides* (maiden pink).

Gardenia. Gardenias are lovely evergreen shrubs with fragrant white flowers that are well suited to the stone and sand garden. Plants need a rather moist soil at all times and prefer a somewhat bright, but not too sunny, place. Recommended are *Gardenia jasminoides*, with double flowers; varieties include 'August Beauty,' 'Radicans,' and 'Veitchii.'

Gentiana. Gentians are low-spreading or upright perennials with

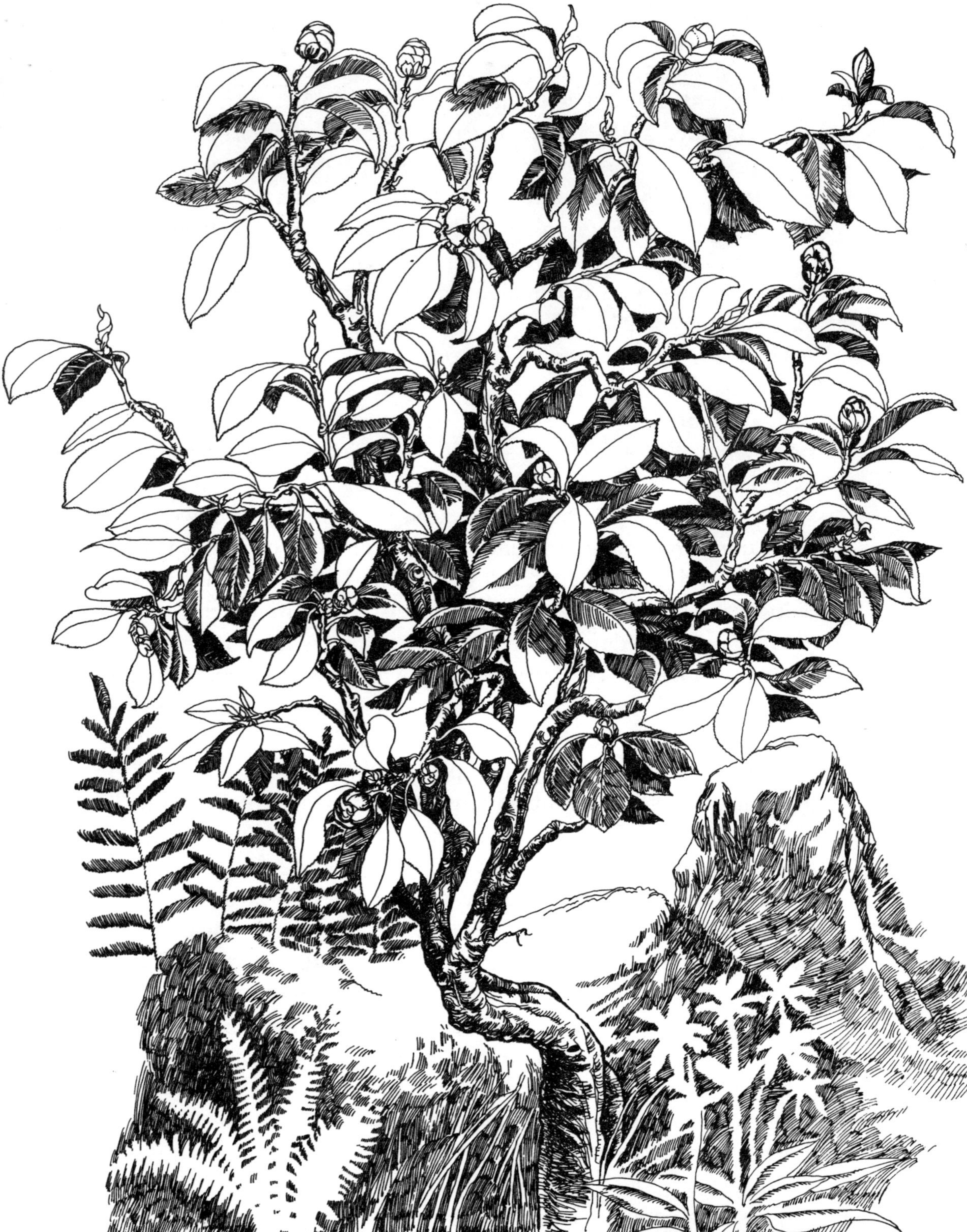

handsome blue tubular flowers that are dramatic in any garden. They are somewhat difficult to grow because they need perfect drainage and a bright, but not too sunny, place; give them ample moisture. Recommended are *Gentiana asclepiadea* and *G. sino-ornata*.

Gypsophila. Gypsophila is a branched upright or spreading annual or perennial. Flowers, borne in summer, are clusters of white, pink, or rose. Grow plants in a somewhat moist situation with plenty of sun. Do not disturb them too often with replanting because they like to stay in one spot. Recommended are *Gypsophila elegans* and *G. paniculata* (baby's breath).

Hibiscus. Hibiscus is a varied group, both deciduous and evergreen, but all blooms are attractive and colorful in a range of pink to red. Plants require good drainage, plenty of sun, and some protection from wind. Recommended are *Hibiscus rosa-sinensis* (any of the varieties) and *H. moscheutos* (perennial hibiscus).

Iris. Iris is an incredibly diverse group of very lovely flowers, with the majority blooming in spring or early summer. Foliage is grasslike, graceful, and ideally suited to the stone and sand garden. There are bulbous iris such as *Iris reticulata* (violet-scented iris) and *I. xiphium* (Spanish iris). Wedgwood iris and Dutch iris are also handsome, but the best is *I. kaempferi* (Japanese iris), which bears blooms of purple, violet, red, or rose and is often edged with contrasting colors. All irises like a moist acid soil and some sunlight.

Lily. Lilies are a popular group of bulbous plants with delicate, colorful blooms. There are innumerable hybrids (too many to list here), but almost all lilies need a deep, loose, well-drained soil, ample moisture year-round, and coolness and shade at the roots. Ask a nurseryman for the recommended varieties in your area.

Peony. The principal classes of peonies are herbaceous and tree peonies. The herbaceous types need a long chilling period. Flowers are from pure white to pale creams and reds. The tree peonies bear very large flowers of incredible beauty, with the Japanese types bearing single or double flowers in shades ranging from white to purple.

Polygonum. Polygonums are a group of evergreen and deciduous perennials with open sprays of white or pink flowers. All need sun to prosper. Recommended are *Polygonum affine* and *P. capitatum*.

Rose. The popular rose is well known and well loved throughout the country. There are hybrid teas, floribundas, grandifloras, miniatures, climbers, old-rose types, and ramblers—an incredible group of wonderful plants. Because there are so many kinds and so many varieties, ask your local nurseryman to recommend plants for your area. To grow plants successfully, buy the best you can afford, locate and plant them properly, and provide water, nutrients, pruning, and pest-and-disease control. Roses do need care, but their flowers "shout" their beauty.

### The Rockery or Mound Garden

The rockery or mound garden is not to be confused with a traditional rock garden. This is a very small scene, handsomely framed with ground covers, small shrubs, or even a bed of flowers. The idea is to set a few handsome rocks in a corner or accent area and contrast them with a light touch of foliage or flower. The scene can be further enhanced with its own carpet of fine gravel.

# 5. Dwarf Plants and Ground Covers

A garden of stone and plants should not be used as an all encompassing landscape. It is best suited to average areas, say about twenty by forty feet. In these places dwarf conifer trees are immensely important; so are the smaller shrubs that are in scale with the landscape.

Ground covers—creepers and mosses—are other plants effectively combined with stone, and they fit in well with hill mounds and rock groupings. Furthermore, like stones and rocks they appear natural in the landscape and can be set in irregular patterns and surfaces that offer color and texture contrasts.

### Dwarf Conifer Trees

Dwarf trees are available in five-gallon cans at nurseries. Have the can cut at the nursery and, if possible, put the tree in the ground the same day. Remove it carefully from the can. Put the plant on its side and slide it from its container; do not pull it out. When you are ready for planting, cradle the root ball in your arms. Do not drag it or pull it around because you want to put as much as possible of the root ball intact into the ground. There will then be a lesser shock to the plant in the transplanting stage.

To plant the conifer, dig a hole about twenty to twenty-four inches; prepare the soil by making it porous and crumbly. Set a mound of soil, center the plant, and fill in halfway with more soil. Water thoroughly and wait about fifteen minutes. Fill the hole with soil and pack in place around the collar of the plant. Leave a concave space at the top, so that water will not wash past the plant. Water thoroughly again.

*Dwarf conifers are in perfect scale to this small garden; the ground covering is gray gravel.* Photo by author.

## Dwarf Plants and Ground Covers

When placing conifers in the stone and sand garden, follow these principles:

1. Use round globe plants for mass and vertical plants for accents.
2. Avoid single plantings.
3. Use groups of the same species.
4. If you mix tree forms, try to arrange them so that there is a balance and scale within that particular group, as though it is a garden in itself.
5. Know the color of the plant; green is not simply green—it is many different hues. Arrange the greens so that they gradually go from light to dark or dark to light.
6. If possible, never use gravel smaller than pea size—about one-half inch in diameter—with conifers.
7. Avoid using colored gravels with conifers; select whites or grays for best results.
8. Never use rocks that will dwarf the plants because the plants are as important as the stones. Select stones that are in scale with the total plantings.

These small plants provide an amazing wealth of texture and color and come in a variety of handsome forms, from round globes to small pyramids. Their beauty, like the rocks and stones they complement, is never ostentatious, but always impressive.

Small conifers are exceedingly valuable in combination with cobbles or, to a somewhat lesser but still attractive degree, gravel. They are excellent for boundary, hill, and mound areas or near paths.

For maximum beauty, plant dwarf evergreens on slight slopes in a staggered staircase arrangement. On level ground and at one height the plants are not as impressive as at levels. Use several trees rather than a solitary specimen, for dwarfs are unattractive alone. You may vary the shapes of the trees—pyramids, globes—in one area, but be careful. The design must be *just* so, two or three of one kind and several of another. In my garden the same kinds are used in one area to present a dramatic grouping, and then differently shaped trees (several) are used in another area to complement the design. If you have the space, repetition of grouping is attractive and creates a feeling of space even in a small garden.

Use texture in the design; there are infinite kinds.

*Dwarf evergreens line a driveway to provide a barrier and a pretty picture. Photo by author.*

*This handsome natural garden uses rocks placed at random with creeping ground covers and some small shrubs and trees. Photo by Clint Bryant.*

*Dwarf shrubs are the background for this handsome rock scene that leads to the house. Photo by Clint Bryant.*

# Dwarf Plants and Ground Covers

Only general suggestions rather than specific cultural rules can be given for these plants. Success depends greatly upon where and how they are grown. Generally, most of the following plants are easy to grow, if given a moderately rich, well-drained soil that is neutral to slightly acid (pH 5 to 7). Most need some sun during the day, although chamaecyparis and cryptomeria do better in light shade.

For new gardens the dwarf conifers and small shrubs are indispensable in the design because they provide scale and accents.

### LIST OF DWARF CONIFER TREES

*Abies balsamea* 'Nana.' Short, flat needles tightly arranged, forming a dense, ball-shaped bushlet.

*Chamaecyparis lawsoniana* 'Forsteckensis' (Forsteck cypress). Blue green ball with branchlets twisted and clustered into cockscombs.

*C. l.* 'Minima.' Stiff, fan-shaped, dark green plumes, blue on underside.

*C. obtusa coralliformis.* Twisted branchlets resembling dark, emerald-green coral.

*C. o.* 'Lycopodioides' (Club-moss cypress). Deep green with blue; develops into a spreading bush.

*C. o.* 'Nana Gracilis' (dwarf Hinoki cypress). Dense fan-shaped branches; slow growing.

*C. pisifera* 'Filifera Nana.' Pale green, long, thin, threadlike branches.

*C. p.* 'Plumosa Minima.' Curly, feathery branchlets; slow growing.

*C. p.* 'Squarrosa Aurea Pygmaea.' Light blue green with golden yellow; forms a dense ball-shaped plant.

*C. p.* 'Squarrosa Cyano Viridis.' Silvery blue green with soft, mossy foliage.

(For other Chamaecyparis, see chapter 6.)

*Cryptomeria japonica* 'Nana.' Stiff and tiny needlelike leaves; slow growing.

*C. j.* 'Vilmoriniana.' Stiff and tiny needlelike leaves; much smaller than *C. japonica* 'Nana.'

*Juniperus chinensis* 'Pfitzeriana Nana.' Irregular spreading, slow-growing bushlet.

*J. c.* 'Plumosa Aurea.' Golden colored, vase-shaped bush.
*J. communis compressa.* Light gray green foliage; slender columnar form.
*J. horizontalis glomerata.* A deep bright green; forms a dense rounded mound.
*J. squamata meyeri.* Bluish white with pink and purple in winter; dense irregular upright grower.
(For more Juniperus, see chapter 4.)

*Picea abies echinaeformis.* Long leaves; slow growing.
*P. a.* 'Procumbens.' A broad flat-topped bushlet.
*P. a.* 'Pumila.' Dense, deep, dark green foliage.
*P. glauca* 'Conica.' Light gray green leaves; dense, narrow conical form.
*Taxus baccata* 'Repandens.' Horizontally spreading branches.
*Taxus cuspidata* 'Minima.' Slow-growing; very dwarf. Dark green needles; tiny leaves.
*Thuja occidentalis* 'Minima.' Light green; turns bronzy in fall. Small and very slow-growing.
*T. o.* 'Ohlendorfii.' Dark bluish green; bronzy in winter.

### List of Dwarf Evergreen Shrubs

*Andromeda polifolia* 'Grandiflora Compacta.' Blue gray, leathery leaves and large pink bells; low, spreading plant.
*A. polifolia* 'Nana.' Low, creeping plant; deep pink bells. Red bronze in winter.
*Berberis buxifolia* 'Nana.' Compact shrub with dark reddish green leaves and large orange flowers.
*B. candidula.* Low and spreading. Hollylike leaves; large orange yellow flowers in spring; black berries in late summer.
*B. stenophylla* 'Nana Compacta.' Blue green, spiny leaves; twiggy growth. Needs protection.
*Bruckenthalia spiculifolia* (Balkan heath). Small, pink, bell-like flowers and sprucelike leaves.
*Buxus microphylla koreana.* Forms a dwarf rounded ball; can be sheared to any shape for formal edgings.
*B. m.* 'Nana Compacta.' Dwarf box with tiny leaves in a tight ball.
*Calluna vulgaris* (many varieties).

## Dwarf Plants and Ground Covers    55

*Cotoneaster horizontalis* 'Little Gem.' Short horizontal branches with shiny green leaves that turn crimson in fall.

*C. microphylla* 'Cooperi.' Textured, tiny evergreen leaves; white flowers and red berries. Slow-growing.

*Daphne cneorum* (garland daphne). Dense arching stems with light leaves; clustering fragrant pink flowers.

*Euonymus fortunei* 'Minima' (dwarf winter creeper). Fine small flowers in spring; tiny evergreen leaves.

*Hebe decumbens.* Tiny gray green leaves; short spikes of white flowers.

*Ilex crenata* 'Helleri' (Japanese holly). Tiny leaves. Sometimes classed as a tree; slow-growing.

*Pieris japonica* 'Compacta.' Dense evergreen bush with white lily-of-the-valley bells.

*P. j.* 'Variegata.' Foliage edged with light yellow; new growth is pink and crimson with subdued yellow. Urn-shaped flowers in early spring. Slow-growing.

*Rhododendron fastigiatum.* Blue green leaves; deep purple flowers in late April.

*R.* 'Gumpo.' Dense, low-growing plant; large white flowers in late spring.

*R. impeditum.* Small leaves; purple blue flowers in early April.

*R. macrantha.* Evergreen, spreading foliage; large pink flowers in May.

*R. macroleucum.* Dense blue green tiny foliage; white flowers in spring.

*R. myrtifolium.* Dark leaves that turn purple bronze in fall; pink flowers in May.

*R. obtusum japonicum.* Lavender pink flowers in late April and May; hardy plant.

*R. racemosum.* Leathery leaves; cherry clusters of flowers in April and May. Slow-growing.

(Also see chapter 6.)

*Salix purpurea* 'Nana.' Finely toothed leaves; lovely shape.

*S. uva-ursi.* Tiny oval leaves with large purple catkins in early spring before leaves appear. Small plant.

*Spiraea bullata.* Rose-colored flowers in midsummer; twelve to fifteen inches high.

*S. compacta arguta.* Slightly taller, with white blooms.

### Ground Covers

To me, ground covers are indispensable in the stone and sand garden; they are infinitely beautiful when well grown, and they help put the finishing touches on the garden. I will generally discuss creepers and mosses rather than the larger ground covers like ajuga, hypericum, and ivy which spread too fast and whose leaves are too large for an intimate feeling in a stone and sand garden. It is the mosses that impart a natural look, for in time they cover stone with beautiful tracery. However, mosses grow slowly and need almost constant shade and moisture, and they are difficult to transplant

*A fine ground cover for rock areas is Thymus Serpyllum.* Photo courtesy of Wayside Garden.

*Sedums are other excellent plants for the rock arrangement.* Photo courtesy of Wayside Garden.

## Dwarf Plants and Ground Covers    57

without the utmost care. In place of tree moss, close-cropped ground cover like wooly thyme, chamomile, Irish moss, and Scotch moss, are ideal.

Put ground covers in place in late fall or early spring, so that they have ideal growing conditions. Plant them at the bases of larger rocks, between stepping-stones, or in crevices—where you want some contrasting color and fine textures. Be sure the ground has a rich soil high in organic matter; use lots of leaf mold and ground bark.

Ground cover plants are sold in flats (sixteen- by twenty-inch wooden boxes). Spade out chunks and set them in place (about six to eight inches apart). Of course, the closer you space them, the quicker they will cover the area. Water the plants with a fine spray; be sure they are thoroughly moistened, since most creepers and mosses thrive on moisture.

Once ground cover starts growing, make sure it does not overgrow stepping-stones or ornamental rocks. It is fine for the cover to extend somewhat up the rocks, but do not allow it to completely engulf the stone. As mentioned, avoid such plants as ivy because they are not part of this garden and always appear out of place.

Ground cover plants are inexpensive and easy to care for, and they come in a variety of textures and forms. Here are only a few of the many available:

### List of Ground Covers

*Alyssum wulfenianum.* Low and compact with grayish foliage.
Antennaria. White wooly gray leaves and tubular flowers.
*Anthemis nobilis* (chamomile). Leaves narrow and linear; grows in almost any soil.
Arabis (rockcress). Handsome white, pink, or purple flowers on small plants.
*Arctostaphylos uva-ursi* (bearberry). Lovely creeper with one-inch leaves and white-on-pink flowers.
*Arenaria verna caespitosa* (Irish moss). Yellow green on dark green leaves; a popular ground cover.
*Asperula odorata* (sweet woodruff). Grows to about eight inches with a spreading habit; fragrant.
*Helxine soleirolii* (baby's tears). Tiny leaves that make a solid green mat; likes shade.

*Herniaria glabra.* Trailing little plant with small green leaves and white flowers; good carpet plant.

*Juniperus conferta.* Spreading shrub with bluish green leaves.

*J. horizontalis.* Tiny trailing branches of bluish green foliage.

*Mentha requienii* (jewel mint of Corsica). Small creeping plant with very small round leaves and pale purple flowers.

*Nepeta hederacea* (ground ivy). Leaves round or kidney-shaped, about one inch across; flowers light blue. Forms a dense mat and can tolerate sun or shade.

*Sagina subulata* (Scotch moss). A densely covered mat with tiny leaves and flowers; rich green. *S. subulata* 'Aurea' is golden green.

*Thymus.* Many species in this group; most have small leaves and prostrate habit.

*Veronica allionii.* Oblong, fine-toothed leaves that form a green carpet.

*V. filiformis.* Small leaves and blue flowers on threadlike stems; prostrate habit.

*V. repens.* A creeping mosslike plant with one-half-inch leaves; white or rose flowers.

# 6. Popular Stone and Sand Garden Plants

Although many kinds of plants are suitable for the stone and sand garden, bamboo, azalea, cypress, and pine are perhaps most seen. These plants are outstanding in line, shape, and texture, and are perfect foils in the stone garden.

Many times a single group of plants used with contrasting plants —such as clumps of bamboo with a few picturesque pines—is all that is needed to complete the beauty of a stone and sand garden. The lacy vertical look of bamboo and the gnarled branches and weathered appearance of pine are all in perfect keeping with stone and sand.

## Popular Stone and Sand Garden Plants

### Bamboo

Bamboo has character and grace; the oriental painters of centuries ago used these plants as painting subjects. Today, placed properly in a garden, bamboo can be as beautiful as depicted in the fine old ink drawings. Bamboo is available in a variety of leaf shapes and heights. Choosing the right variety for the right place is paramount to the total picture.

Bamboos are plants with woody stems divided into sections. Of the two groups of bamboo—running and clumping—the clumping is perhaps the best to work with. As the name suggests, this bamboo grows in clumps and spreads slowly. Unless kept in containers, running bamboo can become vagrant and engulf a garden, so use it with discretion.

Generally, bamboo is a fast-growing plant that is able to withstand wind and rain. It is easy to grow; most kinds will succeed in almost any type of soil and light situation, although for lush growth some sun is necessary. But even though the plants can tolerate untoward conditions and still grow, they will perish quickly without copious watering, especially in spring when new stems appear.

Because of its quick growth, bamboo can be easily trained and pruned to almost any shape. Keep it under control by breaking off tender shoots as they appear. Do not let it grow rampant, for it becomes a tangled mess impossible to train. Prune and shape bamboo early as a young plant, and keep pruning it as you would an espalier.

*Azaleas tie this stone and slate garden together to make an attractive landscape. The azaleas are low-growing and kept trimmed.* Photo courtesy of Buckingham-Virginia Slate Company; Taylor, Lewis & Associates, Architects; Norfolk, Virginia.

*A lone pine in a handsome container is the accent for a garden corner. Pines are popular and easy to train to shape.* Photo by author.

There are bamboos that grow to sixty feet and clumpy kinds; there are small ones and dwarfs, and there are some that have feathery foliage or bolder leaves. Most are graceful, but a few are unattractive.

You can use bamboo in the stone and sand garden in many ways. Clumping bamboo can be used either singly or in groups; smaller types make fine background or filler shrubs. Tall varieties are effective as screens. There are also ground-cover types that range from ten inches (*Sasa pygmae*) to thirty inches (*S. humilis*).

The beauty of bamboo is the strong vertical lines of its stems and the lacy patterns of its leaves. Bamboo is handsome near stepping-stones because it suggests a grove.

Bamboo may not be a capable performer in most climates, but where it can be grown it is indeed a useful plant.

List of Bamboos

*Bambusa multiplex* (hedge bamboo). Can grow to twenty-five feet with dense foliage; hardy to 15°F.

*B. m.* 'Fernleaf.' Handsome ferny bamboo that grows to twenty feet; hardy to 15°F.

*B. m.* 'Golden Goddess.' Grows to ten feet. A popular graceful variety with golden foliage; hardy to 15°F.

*Chimonobambusa quadrangularis* (square-stem bamboo). Attractive with squarish stems and dense foliage. Grows to twenty feet; hardy to 20°F.

*Phyllostachys aurea* (golden bamboo). Rampant grower with stiff stems and dense foliage. Can be contained in tubs; hardy to 20°F.

*P. nigra* (black bamboo). Stems are black. Grows to fifteen feet; hardy to 5°F.

*Sasa disticha* (dwarf fernleaf bamboo). Graceful plant with tiny ferny leaves. Grows to three feet; hardy to 10°F.

*S. humilis* (low bamboo). Graceful arching stems. Grows to three feet; hardy to 0°F.

*S. pygmae* (dwarf bamboo). Rampant grower, but small. Grows to two feet; hardy to 0°F.

Azaleas

Azaleas are only one of the many series in the group Rhododendron. With a wide range of colors, evergreen or deciduous azaleas fit easily into the garden. They are especially good as colorful foils in

# Popular Stone and Sand Garden Plants

the stone and sand landscape. Some plants are small; others can reach to forty feet.

Even when first planted, azaleas have a natural look that makes them appear as if they have always been in a garden. The alpine and dwarf species are effective near stone groups because they have mass and fullness matched by few plants. Generally, low-spreading varieties rather than tall ones are best; taller plants sometimes appear out of scale.

The plants are easy to train and prune, and many have a natural horizontal plane picturesque and attractive in the garden.

Azaleas (and rhododendrons) have infinite uses in the garden—for example, as massed shrubs, hedges, and woodland plantings. Generally, the azalea appears more lightweight than the rhododendron, which tends to be more massive, more bold. When you select your plants, consider them for their use in the garden and also for leaf texture, line, and form.

### Care of Azaleas

Azaleas do not require any more care than other plants, but there are some general rules to follow. Give them a loose porous soil that is somewhat acid in content (pH 4.5 to 6.0) and a cool moist place; some will tolerate some sun, but most varieties prefer shade. Protect the plants from wind; they thrive in a cool humid atmosphere. Above all, provide them with a well-drained soil. Although azaleas, as mentioned, can take some sun, they quickly falter in wind. Thus their transpiration rates increase, so that roots cannot supply additional water as fast as the leaves are losing it. Remember this if you live in a region where soil freezes in winter; the plants simply cannot absorb water from frozen soil and winter winds will kill them.

For best results, plant azaleas in a northern exposure where there is light, but little sun. In a western exposure the afternoon heat may harm plants, and southern locations are too hot for azaleas. Eastern exposures can be successful if mornings are somewhat cloudy. However, early morning sun in winter can damage the frozen leaves and flower buds of early-blooming types by thawing them too rapidly.

As mentioned, use a good porous soil that drains easily, and feed plants with fertilizers on a regular schedule. These are acid-loving plants that need feeding after the first year, sometimes sooner.

List of Azaleas

There are thousands of varieties of azaleas, and although most like shade, newer varieties will tolerate sun. Most are evergreen, and some are deciduous; the majority are easily trained and pruned to shape. Some of the azalea categories are:

*Evergreen*

Belgian Indica. Foliage lush and lovely. Floriferous; hardy to 30°F.
Kaempferi hybrids. Orange red flowers; tall and open growth. Almost leafless in severe winters; hardy to −15°F.
Kurume. Compact and twiggy; densely foliaged with small pretty flowers. Hardy to −5°F.
Macrantha. Low-growing plant, including some fine dwarf varieties. Flowers large; hardy to 5°F.
Pericat. Larger flowers than the Kurumes, but similar in growth and bloom.
Rutherfordiana. Bushy, floriferous plant; hardy to 20°F.
Southern Indica. Will tolerate some sun. Flowers single, double, or semidouble; hardy to 20°F.

*Deciduous*

Knap Hill-Exbury hybrids. Spreading plants to six feet. Clusters of large flowers, white through pink to orange and red; some with contrasting markings.
Mollis hybrids. Upright growth to five feet, with large flowers and colors ranging from chrome yellow to red.
Occidentale hybrids. Tall plants to eight feet, with flowers ranging from pure white to orange.

Pines

Pines are choice plants for stone and sand gardening, and there are several types that can be used advantageously. Pines are evergreen trees, rarely shrubs, and because there are many kinds, it is difficult to give overall cultural rules. Generally, they grow best in a place that has some sun, and, although the soil need not be overly rich, it must be well drained. Needles will yellow if roots become waterlogged.

Pines can have two to five needles to a bundle and can grow from

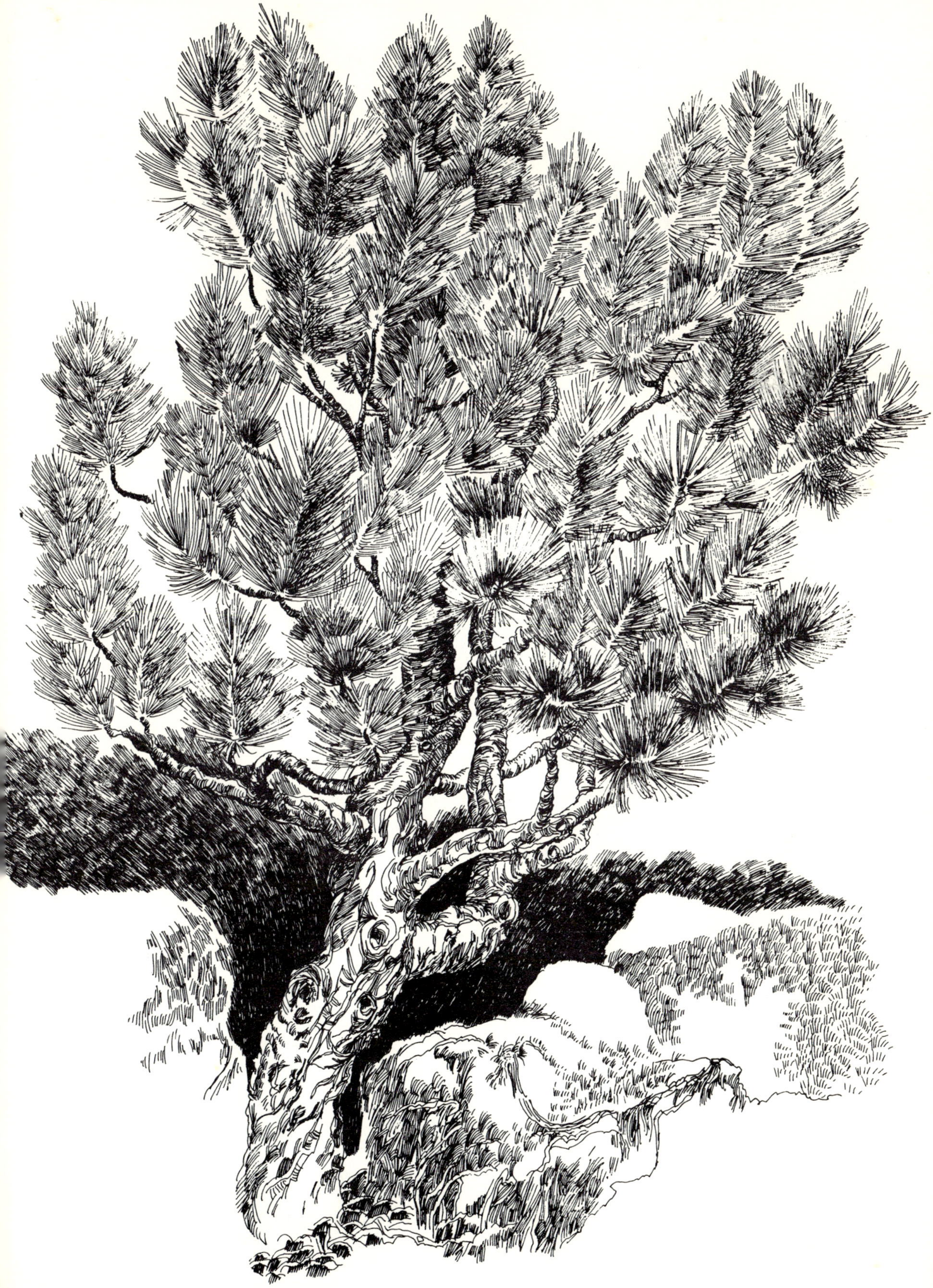

three to eighty feet. The majority are picturesque, with gnarled branches, and are generally slow-growing. They can easily be trained and shaped. Not all pines will be suitable for the stone and sand garden; avoid the upright growers and choose instead the handsome horizontal types.

As single specimens, pines are exceedingly attractive; in groups they seem to lose their beauty. Remember that you are seeking line and form, for the tree is a design element in the garden. Pines are unparalleled in the stone and sand garden when viewed, at their best, from a distance rather than close up. They should be seen as a painting, with the sky as a background. They are framework and must be used with discretion.

List of Pines

*Pinus albicaulis* (whitebark pine). Spreading, generally multitrunked and dense; with dark green needles.

*P. bungeana* (lacebark pine). Spreading habit and picturesque; needles bright green and hardy to subzero.

*P. cembra* (Swiss stone pine). A handsome pyramidal tree with dark green needles; hardy to −35°F.

*P. contorta* (shore pine). Contorted in growth and dwarf; ideal in the stone and sand garden. Dense green foliage; hardy to −35°F.

*P. densiflora* (Japanese red pine). Broad, irregularly shaped tree with blue green or yellow green needles; hardy to −20°F.

*Shaped and trained trees are part of the oriental garden. The tree against the house is trained to a disc pattern; note that it is the negative areas between the branches that make the design so pleasing. Photo by author.*

# Popular Stone and Sand Garden Plants

- *P. d.* 'Umbraculifera' (tanyosho pine). A broad, flat-topped, multi-trunked tree with blue green or yellow green needles; hardy to −20°F.
- *P. edulis* (nut pine). Fine small-branching pine with dark green, dense, and stiff needles; hardy to −10°F.
- *P. mugo* (Swiss mountain pine). A bushy, small, pyramidal tree with dense, dark green needles; hardy.
- *P. m. mughus* (Mugho pine). Popular because it only grows to four feet. Dark green needles; very hardy.
- *P. nigra* (Austrian black pine). A dense tree with branches in whorls. Stiff dark green needles; very hardy.
- *P. parviflora* (Japanese white pine). A pyramidal tree with gray blue to green needles; hardy to −20°F.
- *P. radiata* (Monterey pine). Fast-growing and picturesque with bright green needles; hardy to −15°F.
- *P. strobus* 'Nana' (dwarf white pine). A broad and bushy tree with blue green needles; a good one and hardy.
- *P. thunbergii* (Japanese black pine). Spreading branches with bright green needles. Easily trained; outstanding and hardy.

### CHAMAECYPARIS

Chamaecyparis—evergreen trees and shrubs with many varieties and color forms—is called false cypress. The plants are highly prized for gardens because they are easily trained to sculptural shapes and are relatively free of pests and disease. Of the Japanese species *Chamaecyparis obtusa* and *C. pisifera* there are many varieties under various names, and nomenclature of the group is confusing. For complete satisfaction and the kind of tree you want, consult the following lists and then visit a local nursery to make selections.

Grow false cypress in a fast-draining soil, since they are prone to root rot in clayey soils. Trim and pinch plants frequently, for without attention they tend to grow straggly. Select a bright place for them; they will not prosper in shade. In the northern part of the country some cypress tend to turn brownish in the winter.

The following trees are only a sampling of the many varieties:

### LIST OF CHAMAECYPARIS

*Chamaecyparis lawsoniana* 'Aurea.' Grows to six feet; silver gray blue with pyramidal form and drooping branches.

*C. obtusa* (Hinoki false cypress). Grows to forty feet; dark glossy green with irregular spreading form. Easily pruned to shape.

*C. o.* 'Aurea' (golden Hinoki cypress). Grows to thirty feet. Golden foliage when young, dark green when mature; picturesque.

*C. o.* 'Filicoides' (fernspray cypress). Grows to fifteen feet. Medium green with dense foliage and short frondlike branches; a graceful tree.

*C. o.* 'Torulosa.' Grows to three feet, with twisted threadlike branches; slow-growing and lovely.

*C. pisifera* (Sawara false cypress). Grows to twenty feet, with dark green foliage and open growth. Prune heavily to shape; outstanding.

*C. p.* 'Filifera' (thread cypress). Grows to ten feet, with dense green foliage and weeping twigs; handsome.

M. VALDEZ 3 '71

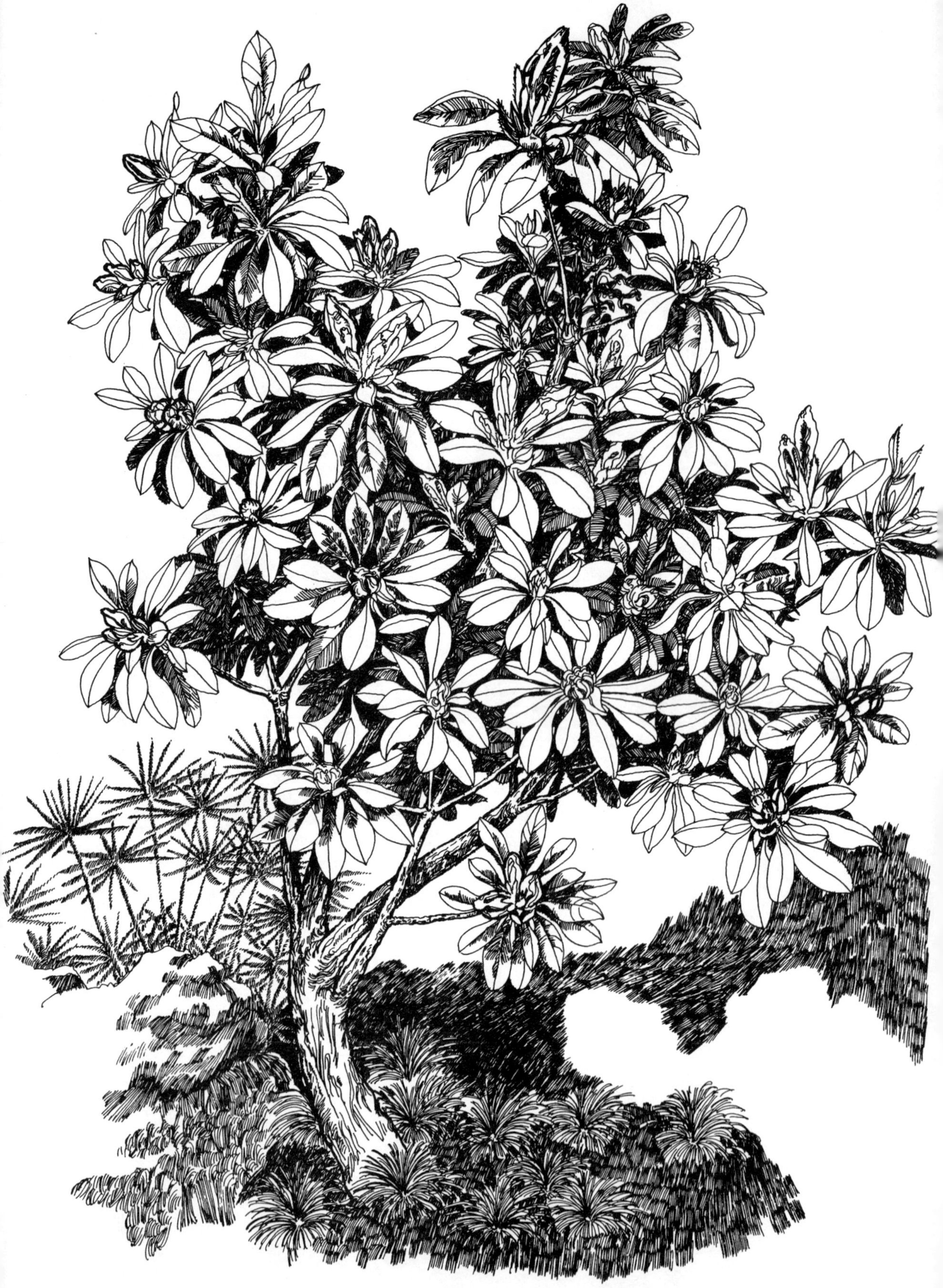

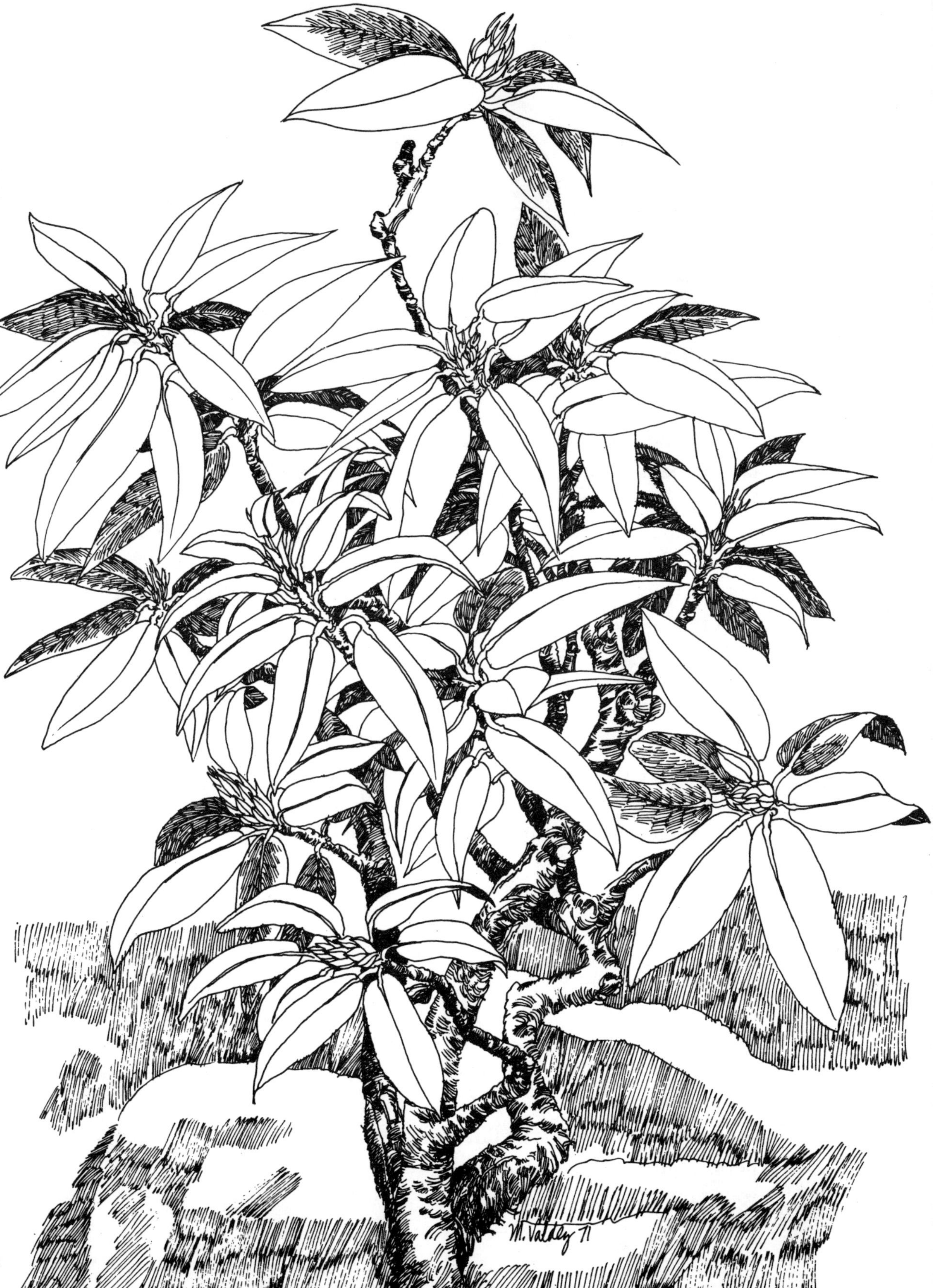

# 7. Paths and Stepping-Stones

Paths and walks in your garden are more important than you might think. They not only should be a means of moving through the landscape, but should also be esthetically pleasing and add a design element in the garden. Indeed, without paths or stepping-stones, a garden may often appear bleak and uninviting. It is the paths and the materials used for them—stepping-stones, concrete rounds, gravel, wood, earth—that complete the whole and tie the landscape picture together.

There are three kinds of paths: natural paths that develop from casual walking—the ground gets packed down and then is filled with gravel or fir bark; paved paths of brick, asphalt, or concrete; and paths of stepping-stones.

Each type of path has its use in the garden, and which you choose depends on the garden itself—size and shape—and the character of the garden. Stepping-stones generally look best, but gravel paths are acceptable too.

### Simple Paths

The most natural path is earthen; its construction is simple. Soak the soil thoroughly, and strip at least two inches of soil off the top, removing weeds and grass roots. Cut the path about four feet wide and level it. Firm the earth in place. Make the path slightly higher in the center than at the edges, so that water will not accumulate in the center where you walk. Use a roller to compact the soil; compact several times until it is well tamped down. Weeds have to be removed periodically, and, if the path gets too rough, it has to be sprinkled and rolled down again.

Gravel paths also require only simple installation, and gravel has advantages over other surfacing materials. Dirt spilled on gravel can be washed away without fuss; a gravel path dries quickly, and water from rain or hosing does not accumulate on the path. There are endless patterns you can use; all are easy to install, since gravel is a workable material. Its only disadvantage is that leaves adhere to it, which makes raking almost impossible.

Install a gravel path with a permanent bedrock or decomposed granite underneath. Then put down a polyethylene sheet to keep out weeds. Perforate the sheet, so that water can drain away. Generally, gravel paths require header boards or brick borders to keep them in place. Simply install trenches with a two-by-four board on edge after you dig the path.

Roll the gravel in place with a roller, and then rake the stones over the area in thin layers, dampen, and roll again. Repeat the process until the path is built up to the final thickness. Use one-half-inch pebbles; anything smaller will be kicked away, and anything larger will be difficult to walk on.

Stepping-stones can also be used in combination with gravel, and in that case put them in first, omitting header boards or borders. Allow the path a more open feeling, and let it mingle with the ground cover along the edges. Gravel may slow you down when you walk, but there is no need to hurry through a lovely garden, and the sound of gravel underfoot is always pleasing.

Fir bark makes a springy path and is becoming more popular. It is an inexpensive material, easy to apply, and, like gravel, it can be put down in many designs without undue effort. However, most wood-chip and fir-bark paths need to be replaced every year since they naturally deteriorate, and, if drainage is not good, bacteria or insect infection can occur.

Choose one-half- or one-inch diameter fir bark for paths; smaller grade will wash away, and larger grade is uncomfortable to walk on. About three cubic yards of fir bark will cover a two-hundred-square foot area to a depth of two inches.

### Stepping-Stones

Stone paths are classic and, to me, the most pleasing in the garden. They come in a variety of sizes and kinds, can be used in many de-

*Flat-topped rocks provide a path through a rose garden; they are spaced at random, but not so far apart to make walking difficult. Photo by Roche.*

*Cobbles line a concrete path; the arc design and placement of the stones create a fine study in textures. Photo by Clint Bryant.*

signs, may be placed at various levels, and are generally easy to work with. Furthermore, unlike gravel or fir bark, which has to be replaced periodically, stone remains for years and weathers with a lovely patina.

Select natural rocks with a flat surface or use commercial cast-form types or a combination of the two. Old mill stones, granite slabs, or stone piers are also effective. But no matter what kind of stone you select, be sure it is large enough to accommodate a person's foot.

The shortest distance between two points may be a straight line, but avoid this rule if you are using stepping-stones in the garden, because a straight path divides an area and makes it seem smaller than it is. An arrow-straight path rarely looks good; curving and random paths blend in much better with a outdoor scene. S-curves, staggered arrangements, or irregular curves are all possibilities when working with stone. A path should wander among the trees and around large rocks, under branches and near shrub clumps. Use some imagination when installing stone paths, and your garden will greatly benefit.

Make gradual turns in the path; never make abrupt turns, for in a garden of repose sudden changes are distracting. Since there are so many variations with stepping-stones, it is impossible to set forth rigid rules, but one guideline should be followed: a path should have

## Paths and Stepping-Stones 73

a recognizable unity. There should be a linking theme throughout.

Large stones and small stones can be effectively used together, as can round and long ones, and so on. The stepping-stone path is man-made, but, like the garden, it should appear natural, as if it has been there for many years.

### Installing Stepping-Stones

Space stone paths at comfortable distances, so that people don't have to take long strides. Stones too far apart are difficult to walk on in wet weather. Each stone should relate to its companion stone. Like the stones in the garden, stepping-stones should have good character and texture. Be sure to use stones large enough for the foot, but not so large that they conflict with the other stones in the garden. Avoid using same-sized stones in a path; vary them enough to add interest and yet retain harmony.

*Round stepping-stones in an alternating pattern is the entrance to this house.* Photo by Clint Bryant.

*Cobbles in concrete form a small bridge over a simulated water scene using smaller cobbles.* Photo by author.

**raised above bed of pebbles**

**path through groundcover**

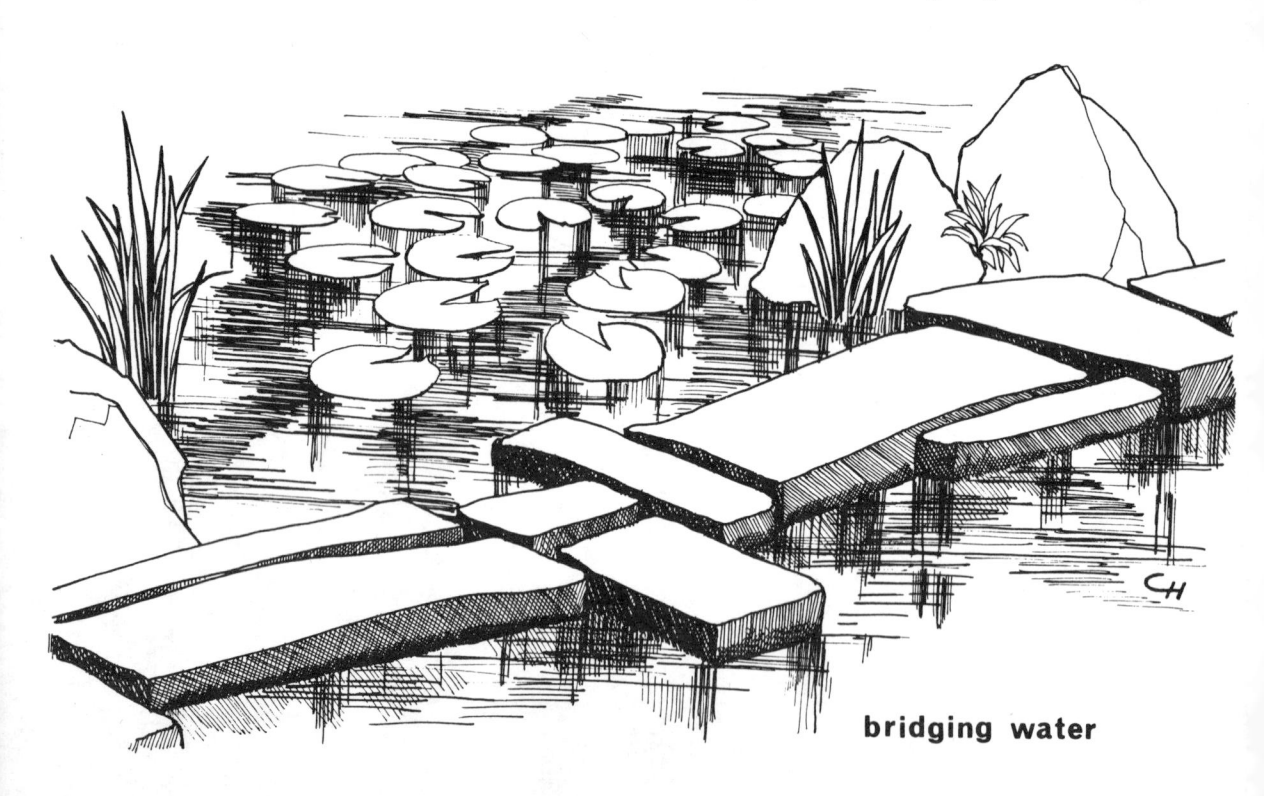

**bridging water**

# STEPPING STONES

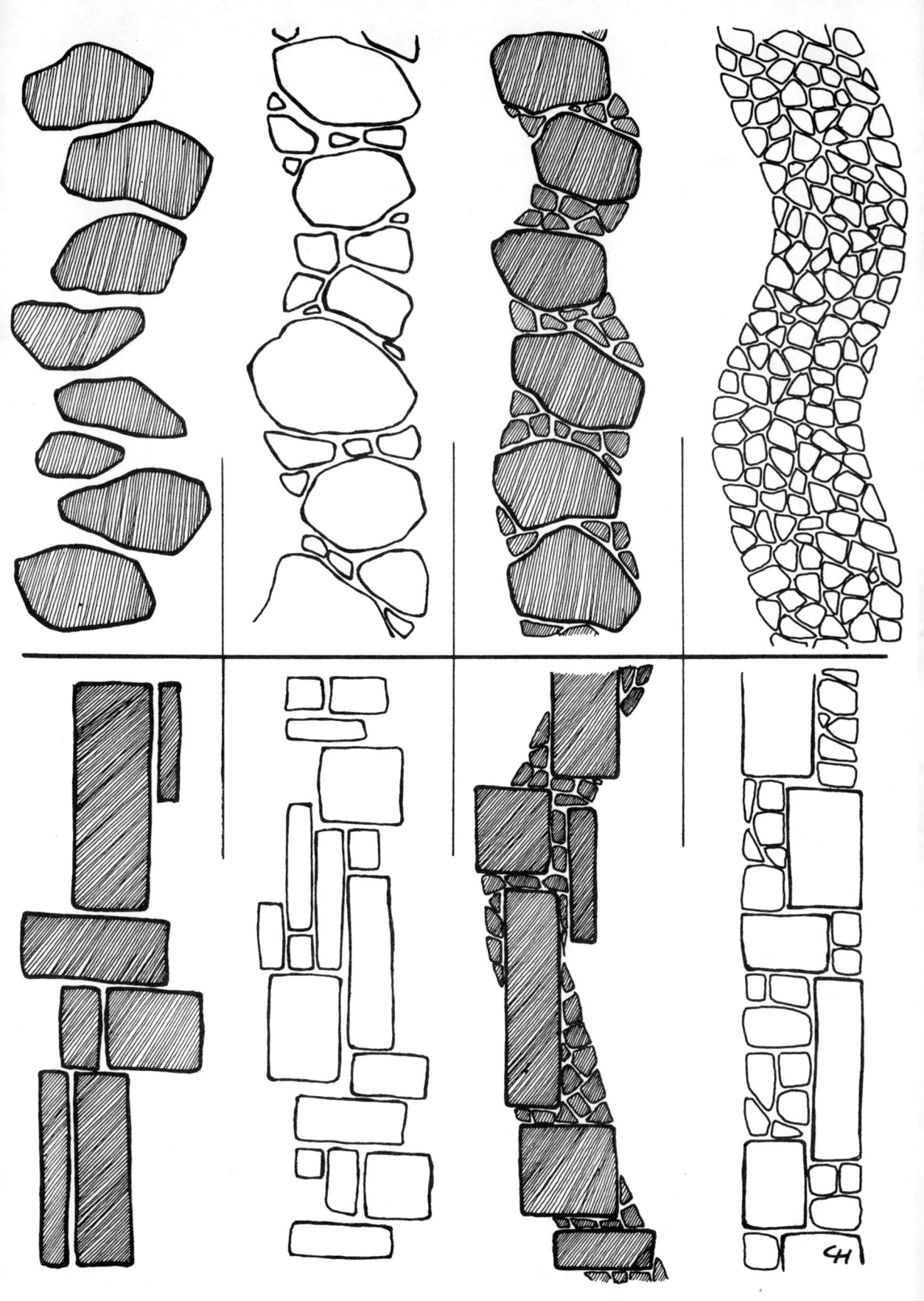

**STEPPING STONE PATTERNS**

Use larger stones to denote intersections in a path. Generally, stones should be laid broadside across a path rather than lengthwise to it. Paths with stones pointing in the direction of the path tend to hurry you along; stone paths with stones perpendicular to the axis of the path are more comfortable in appearance. Above all, be sure to set each stone in place firmly by burying at least two-thirds of it for stability, and be sure each stone is set so that its surface is level. The base may be irregular since it is buried, but the top should be reasonably flat.

To lay out a stone path, use a length of rope or garden hose on the ground in the design you want. (Decide on the arrangement and draw shapes on paper until a pleasing design is found.) Place the primary or largest stones first; work in the secondary or smaller ones later. Lay the stones in a concrete base or on a sand or soil subbase. Remember that stones should be slightly higher than ground level to prevent the soil from working over them.

# 8. Water in the Garden

Water in small amounts—pool, dish, basin—is to the stone and sand garden what flowers are to a traditional garden; it completes the natural scene. Natural streams, waterfalls, and ponds are generally beyond today's garden because there is rarely enough space for them and large water areas require a great deal of care. However, small prefabricated pools and dishes of water can easily be added without exorbitant cost or labor. Water is not only pleasing to see but soothing to hear, since it can sound like a soft ripple or a whispering jet. It mirrors the sky and provides a screen for reflected images of tree and branch. And water makes an area seem cooler.

The decision to add water to the garden depends on your individual tastes, but remember that, when you introduce water to the garden, you also open the door to the fascinating world of water plants. Lilies and lotus, rushes and grasses, iris and bamboo are graceful and beautiful plants that are hard to resist.

*A beautiful arrangement of cobbles provides interest around a fountain. Photo by Jim Kenney; courtesy of Longue Vue Gardens.*

*Natural stones line this small water pool; the stones, only recently placed, seem as if they have been there for years. Photo courtesy of Architectural Pottery.*

When we speak of water in the garden, we mean natural ponds and pools. Traditional pools in the manner of the grand chateaux or impressive waterfalls are not suitable for our purposes. Our water accent is in shallow bowls or man-made, small, natural pools.

Pools and Ponds

Make a small pool by digging a hole and sinking a watertight container, such as a laundry tub or a photographer's tray, into the ground. Free-form polyethylene pools that can be installed in the same manner as the commercial dishes are also available. Still another type of pool is a heavy gauge plastic sheet; dig a hole, spread the plastic over it, and fill with water.

Pools that look best, however, are generally made from a concrete shell. Lay out on the ground the general line of the pool. Excavate the site to about twenty-four inches, making sloping sides. Dig trenches for a drain, so that the pool can be emptied without trouble. Cover the trenches with soil, and line them with about two inches of gravel tamped down. Spread reinforcing or chicken wire over the bottom of the site and pour the concrete. The gravel will eliminate possible cracking of the shell by settling the soil, particularly in cold-weather areas where soil freezes and thaws.

Now put in a four- or five-inch layer of concrete. The mix should

*Here cobbles are used to simulate water under a small bridge; the placement of cobbles must be perfect to create the illusion.* Photo by author.

*Large stones are used here to provide make-believe water course.* Photo by author.

be heavy, so that it is easy to trowel up the sides of the excavation. Do the pouring in one continuous operation, so that there will be no joints for water to seep through. Trowel the mix to a rough surface after it is poured.

Cure the pool if it is to have plants or fish. Fill the new pool with water and let it stand for twenty-four hours. Drain, refill, and repeat three or four times. After the last time allow the water to stand for about a week, then rinse the pool thoroughly and refill; it is now ready for fish or plants.

Around the pool set rocks and stone in place, so that all exposed edges are hidden. You want the pool to look as natural as possible, so make it appear as if it has been there for some time.

Avoid an isolated spot of water, for it is rarely attractive; plants are what make this garden live. To get you started, here are some water plants. (For a full discussion of care and culture and other aquatics, see the book *Water Gardening*, a companion guide in this series.)

### Plants for Water Gardens

Water with a green accent, stone, and sand naturally go together, and with a judicious use of materials the water garden can be stunning. Just how you put it together is the key to success. Balance and scale between plants and water is what you should strive for, and harmony of materials is the link that can make the ordinary garden extraordinary.

Group plants in sweeps around the pool, but do not have so many that they become a jungle. Each should stand by itself and yet blend with the landscape. Graceful plants, like rushes, grasses, and cattails, supply vertical accent; lush plants with rich green foliage, such as taro and water arum, supply mass and volume. For color around the pool use iris and marsh marigolds; floating plants in the pool will provide drama. Lotus and water lilies are showy and put on a glorious summer display.

### Plants around the Pool

Border plants grow in any good heavy loam and need little attention. Putting them in place at their proper planting level is important. Some like their root crowns just slightly above water level; others must have roots in marshy soil. Several need six to ten inches of water above the crown of the plant.

*Acorus calamus* (sweet flag). A hardy perennial that likes shallow water. Has broad, dark green leaves to three feet.
*Caltha palustris* (marsh marigold). Sometimes called buttercup; has notched leaves and lovely waxy yellow flowers. Needs water crown barely under water.
*Cyperus papyrus* (Egyptian paper plant). Has fronds of thready umbrellalike leaflets at the ends of bending stems; needs two to three inches of water. *Cyperus alternifolius* is also desirable.
*Equisetum hiemale* (horsetail). A fine vertical accent with colorful stalks; needs one to four inches of water.

*Hosta plantaginea* (plantain lily). Desirable, large, heart-shaped leaves. Spreads rapidly in shallow water.

Iris. A large family with many beardless irises that grow well in heavy, moist soil. *Iris versicolor* is the popular and exquisite blue species. *I. kaempferi* (Japanese iris) bears brilliant purple blooms, and *I. sibirica* (Siberian iris) has blue purple flowers. All need sun.

Sagittaria (arrowhead). A popular poolside plant with dark green leaves; grows to four feet and needs a wet soil or water to six inches in depth. *Sagittaria latifolia* (common arrowhead) and *S. sagittifolia* (giant arrowhead) are generally available from suppliers.

Thalia (water canna). Bold spear-shaped foliage and deep purple flowers. Flourishes in an inch or so of water.

*Typha latifolia* (cattail). A common bog plant that grows to six feet with dark brown tails. Needs about six inches of water. *Typha latifolia* is called common cattail. *T. angustifolia* (common cattail) is shorter with narrow leaves, and *T. minima* (pygmy cattail) grows to only twelve inches.

### Floating Plants for the Pool

*Aponogeton distachyus* (water hawthorn). A winter-flowering aquatic with tiny white flowers.

*Azolla caroliniana*. A mosslike plant with tiny scalloped leaves. Forms a water carpet of dull green to dark red in sun.

*Eichhornia crassipes* (water hyacinth). Has inflated leafstalks and erect leaves. Lovely violet flowers with a yellow eye. *E. azurea* has purplish blue blooms.

*Hottonia palustris* (water violet). Charming plant with loose spikes of mauve flowers.

*Hydrocleis nymphoides* (water poppy). A charming small plant that looks like a water lily. Bears yellow flowers almost all year in warm climates. Needs only about five inches of water.

Nelumbo (lotus). Thick stems and handsome round leaves; incredibly large and stunning flowers. Grows in shallow boxes of soil and manure; needs about ten inches of water. Many varieties.

*Pistia stratiotes* (water lettuce). Floats on the surface of the pool. Has trailing, long, hairlike roots and resembles garden lettuce.

Salvinia. Heart-shaped with tiny, hairy leaves. Grows vigorously.

### Water Lilies

Water lilies are extremely beautiful, but not difficult to grow. If

## Water in the Garden

properly planted at the start, they are amenable subjects that need little attention.

This is a large group of plants and new varieties are introduced frequently. The flowers are magnificent, some twelve inches across, and they come in vibrant colors. There are hardy water lilies and tropical ones; the latter have the largest flowers and are treated as annuals—planted in late spring or early summer and discarded in the fall. Some bloom during the day and others open at night; many are very fragrant. Several varieties carry their blooms above the surface of the water. Their foliage is luxuriant, and many have toothed or fluted leaves. But even if you have a greenhouse, it will be almost impossible to carry over tropicals through winter.

The hardy water lilies bloom during the day and last about three days. Generally they float on the surface of the water, and the flowers are smaller than the tropicals. A few varieties bear stalks somewhat above the surface of the water. At the first frost hardy lilies die back and winter safely under ice, provided the pool depth is at least twenty-eight inches; then in spring they come back with fresh growth.

For water lilies (both kinds) the pools should be at least twenty inches deep (thirty inches is better). The plants require a great deal of sun, so do not expect them to be floriferous in shade. They need rich soil and plenty of fertilizer, especially the tropicals, which have a short period of growth. Rather than planting the lilies at the bottom of the pool, I find it better to work with them in pine planter boxes. Do not use redwood boxes, as the wood will turn water black and may kill plants. For container growing put in an eight- to ten-inch bed of fertilizer and rich soil. Do not mix the ingredients or use sand. Anchor the container to the bottom of the pool by mooring wires to a brick, or use a wooden batten to keep the box from floating.

Hardy lilies are available at suppliers about mid-April (depending on where you live) either as a piece of rootstock with leaves and perhaps a few buds or just a section of rootstock. Tropicals are set out later in the season, sometime about mid-June, and should be planted when water temperature is about 70°F.

Plant both kinds of lilies as soon as you get them, so that they do not dry out, which might hinder or prevent new growth. If you cannot plant them immediately, keep them in a shady place out of the sun because even an hour of bright light may harm them.

**NYMPHAEACEAE** Nymphaea (Water lily)

**NYMPHAEACEAE** Nelumbium (Water lotus)

I have not included a list of water lilies because there are so many and color choice is a matter of personal taste. Catalogs from suppliers list many varieties of water lilies.

### Ways to Suggest Water in the Garden

The water garden need not be exactly what it says; the scene might only suggest water. This simulation is done with stones arranged in wavy patterns. From a distance the effect is pure trickery, for, if the stones are installed properly, the viewer will think there is water where there is not.

The waterless garden is made by excavating a shallow depression in the earth; this area is then lined with flat stones of uniform size in intricate patterns to suggest water. The stones must be perfectly placed, or the garden does not come off properly. Fine gravel can be used to represent islands or stepping-stones. Along the edges of the area more stones can be placed to indicate the bank. Streams and ponds can be hinted at by using groups of stones on a small hill, or you can plan a winding course going through the garden from high to low ground with pebbles arranged in a meandering pattern. Larger rocks along the edges and some grassy plants complete the picture.

The *effect* of having water in the garden without *really* having it depends on the arrangement of each pebble. It is a procedure that must be followed with infinite patience and care. Flat circular stones laid closely together will suggest water, as will elongated stones pointed in one direction.

# 9. Maintenance and Pest Control

The stone and sand garden by its very nature is easy to care for. There are no flower beds to keep you in constant motion and, because there are generally few plants, pests and disease are not often seen. Maintenance consists of periodically shaping plants and keeping gravel areas free of leaves or debris. Stone and rock never need attention; neither does sand, although occasional replenishing might be necessary.

PLANT PROTECTION

In spring and fall make a routine cleanup of the garden. Put in new gravel or sand if it is necessary, and pinch new growths on plants to head them in the right direction. Remove deadwood and dried foliage. Support and stake plants that need it. Make a thorough cleanup of weeds that might have started growth.

If you are going to put a new plant in the garden or transplant an established one, do it in spring (if you are in cold winter regions) when good weather is on the way. In mild climates early fall is the time for transplanting.

Be sure the garden area is clear of all trash; this eyesore mars the beauty of the stone and sand garden. Debris also provides breeding places for many insects, so it should be removed immediately. Generally with routine care and careful observation, plants will rarely be attacked by insects.

Observe shrubs and trees as you walk in the garden. If leaves are limp or growth is poor, look to cultural conditions first rather than suspecting insects. Are plants getting enough or too much light? Are they getting ample water?

Use mulches for your plants; they are a tremendous labor saver and water saver. A mulch specifically keeps moisture around the roots of the plants, and saves water. It also smothers weeds before they have a chance to grow, and it helps to keep the soil friable. Mulches also keep the soil from freezing and thawing in the fall and early spring, so that plants are not heaved from the ground.

There are several organic mulches, such as leaves, peat, pecan shells, ground tree bark, sawdust, and peanut shells. Inorganic mulches are aluminum foil, fiberglass-insulation, and stones. Small pebbles make excellent mulches and blend into the stone and sand garden. The stones allow water to go through the soil quickly and still protect the soil and plant roots. Apply the pebbles in handsome patterns around plants.

Apply mulches after the soil has had a chance to warm up in spring and growth has started. In fall they can be put in place after soil has frozen.

# Maintenance and Pest Control

### Protection against Insects

Many insects and plant diseases are brought in with soil. Because the stone and sand garden contains little soil, insects are rarely a problem. However, if you do find them on shrubs or trees, do not panic. They are easily eliminated—and without poisons—if they are detected early.

Your first line of defense is birds; several kinds of birds consume insects by the pound. Ladybugs and praying mantises are voracious insect eaters, and these beneficial critters are now available from suppliers. Lacewings also devour harmful bugs.

A strong hose of water will deter aphids and mealybugs. Small caps of beer will discourage snails and slugs. Leafhoppers, thrips, caterpillars, and whiteflies can be controlled with safe botanical sprays containing pyrethrum or rotenone, nature's own insecticide derived from plants.

If, however, a severe infestation of insects occurs, there are some synthetic poisons said to be nonpersistent in the soil; these include Malathion and Diazinon. However, I do not recommend their use, and they are cited here only as a last resort.

If this chapter seems brief, it is because stone and sand gardens simply do not harbor the kind of pests you find in the usual garden. As mentioned at the start of this book, once the garden is installed, care is really at a minimum and pleasure is always maximum.